Child's Play

Lynda Madaras

Peace Press

Published and Printed by Peace Press, Inc.
3828 Willat Avenue
Culver City, California 90230

First Edition

Madaras, Lynda.
  Child's Play.

  1. Play—United States.   2. Play groups—United
States.   I. Title
HQ782.M32   649'.5   76-50118
ISBN 0-915238-09-8

Cover Design: William I. Teitelbaum
Cover Drawing: Area Madaras
Illustrations: Jared Martin, Christian Martin, Area Madaras,
          Lynda Madaras, George Madaras
Layout: Jared Martin, Lynda Madaras, Bonnie Mettler
Photos: Lynda Madaras, Cindy Olsen
Back Cover Photo: Lavalais

This book is dedicated to Elmo which was how my brother Albert referred to my daughter before she was born. Once she was born we never could decide on a name which really annoyed the lady at the Bureau of Vital Statistics who called every morning for three weeks. In the end, we decided to let her pick her own name. At times it was a little strange—like when she decided her name was Volkswagon. However, when she was about three she came up with the name Area and it stuck. So really, this book is dedicated to Area Madaras my much loved daughter who is one of the finest souls I have ever come across.

THANK YOUS

For starters I'd like to thank Christian Martin because I promised him I would. I also had to promise to put his picture in the book. That's him in the margin. He did the drawings on pages 5, 6, 25, 26, 35, 36, 39, 40, 55, 63, 64, 75, 76 & 94. But even if I hadn't promised him I'd have done it anyhow because he worked really hard and came up with some magnificent drawings. Besides he named his cat after me. The cat unfortunately jumped out the window of a nine-story apartment building. Twice. The second jump was the last jump. Still, I appreciated the thought.

Then, too, I want to thank my daughter Area who did the drawing on the cover as well as some of the photos and drawings on the inside of the book. Thanks also to Simon and Demetri Elbling who drew ants; Tybelle Carson who drew a lovely princess; the kids in Pam Rousseau's class at Sequoyah School and the kids at the Pasadena Arts Workshop who also drew heaps of pictures for me; Jenny Worth and Seth Darling who let me use their stories and pictures; Dane Saavedra who let me use his picture puzzle; Dickie Lavalais who took the picture on the back cover; Cindy Olsen who did the photos on pages 29, 31, 34, 99, 123, 132 and 135; Bonnie Mettler who did the paste-up and filled up the blank spots here and there with a drawing or two; Ann Worth who typed the manuscript and corrected my atrocious spelling; all the people at Peace Press who published and printed the book—especially Harold Moskovitz who put up with me.

Special thanks to Jared Martin who put in many long hours designing the layout and doing illustrations. Of course, I wouldn't want to forget to thank my crazy Hungarian erstwhile husband for the illustrations in the last-part of the book. And perhaps the most important people to thank are the members of the Dirty Feet Playgroup: Jimmy, Susan and Dana Carson; Seth and Caryn Darling; Sara and Michael Hennesy; Lynda, George and Area Madaras; Tim and Bridget Morton; Katie and Dane Saavedra; Margie and David Seal; Shawn and Sol Slavin; Steve, Ann, Jenny and Peter Worth; Colette, Jeffrey and Jason Van Cleve. Thanks to all of you.

Lynda Madaras
March 1977

P.S. I would be remiss if I did not mention the continued encouragement and inspiration of Otis Young who read the manuscript and said he was hardly bored at all.

CONTENTS

Yogurt Carton Puppets • Cloth Puppets • Puppet Theatres

Playgroups

We have a lot of very curious beliefs in our culture. One particularly peculiar notion is that *the very best* way to raise kids is to have them spend the first five years of their lives at home with their mothers. It is peculiar because every mother and every kid knows that staying home together, day in and day out, for those five years is guaranteed to bore any kid out of his skull and drive mothers up a wall. Yet, until recently, childcare outside the home was looked upon as a necessary evil—only for families where death, divorce or dire economic straits forced the mother to abandon her "natural" role and go to work.* Young children of working mothers were objects of pity, poor waifs. The selfish hussy who actually *chose* to go out and get a job had to deal with all sorts of cultural bugaboos. Even the liberal Dr. Spock let us know that the children of working mothers were subject to bedwetting, separation traumas, and all sorts of psychological calamities (guilt! guilt!).

But times are changing and things are looking up. Dr. Spock has eaten his words. The newly revised edition of his baby rearing bible reveals a whole new attitude. Families are changing as well. Instead of staying at home, many moms are going back to school, taking paying jobs, or simply realizing that they deserve a break from the twenty-four-hour-a-day job of mother and homemaker. In some few brave families, dads are taking over the childcare job. There is also an increasing number of single-parent families who need childcare. The traditional program—mom and the kids at home—just doesn't work for these modern families. People are deciding that the old way may not be the very best way after all. Rather than thinking of childcare outside the home as a necessary evil, we are realizing that childcare programs may be a healthier alternative. Kids who have the opportunity to spend time with other adults, in other environments, and play with a wider circle of friends, opportunities that childcare programs can offer, may be fuller, happier, more creative human beings for it.

*Go to work meaning, of course, taking a paying job outside the home because as everybody knows housewives do not work. They lounge around all day eating cherry bon bons.

This positive attitude towards childcare creates its own problems, though. There simply aren't enough childcare facilities for all the parents and kids who need them. In 1970 there were over 5 million children under the age of six whose mothers worked (at paying jobs). Yet the Daycare and Child Development Council of America reported only 700,000 children in licensed daycare facilities. What were the other 4,300,000 kids doing while their moms were working? Some of them were simply left to fend for themselves. Others were cared for by neighbors, friends, relatives, or older siblings. Obviously a lot of these kids did not have adequate supervision. Many had no playmates their own age, yet kids need other kids. They need to share their fears and fantasies and to learn how to get along with others.

Yet, as the figures suggest, trying to find a good childcare program that will provide adequate supervision, playmates and a stimulating environment is not easy. The waiting lists at most childcare centers are ridiculous. At one particularly good center in my area, pregnant women sign up their unborn babies so that their children will have a chance to get in by the time they are three years old!

Even those lucky enough to find space in a good center may discover that the center's hours are wrong, its location too far away, or their kids too young. Many childcare programs will not accept kids under the age of three. Some programs will not take kids on a part-time basis; others are *only* open part-time. Parents who work odd hours may find that the center opens too late or closes too early to accommodate their schedules.

The biggest obstacle for families who want good childcare is money. Childcare is expensive. Fees run anywhere from $100 (cheap) to $200 or more a month. For low and moderate income families these fees are prohibitive. Even fairly affluent families may be strapped by the high cost of childcare, especially if they have more than one child. There are mothers who literally cannot afford to take a job. By the time they pay for the necessary clothes, transportation, taxes and childcare, it actually *costs* them to have a paying job.

One solution for at least some of these parents and kids: Playgroups. Playgroups are a bunch of kids who play together regularly and whose parents share the childcare responsibility: a sort of do-it-yourself child-

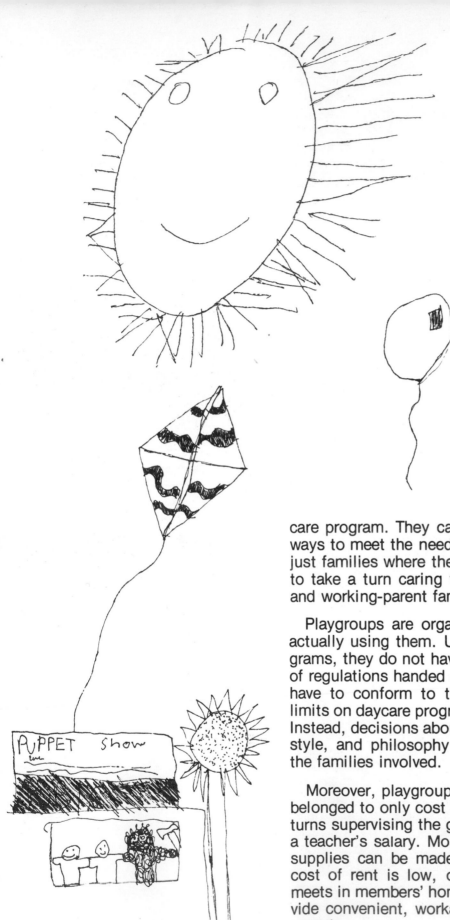

care program. They can be set up in a multitude of ways to meet the needs of all kinds of families—not just families where the mom is home during the day to take a turn caring for the kids, but single-parent and working-parent families as well.

Playgroups are organized by the people who are actually using them. Unlike government funded programs, they do not have to adhere to an arbitrary set of regulations handed down from above. Nor do they have to conform to the dictates of profit that set limits on daycare programs run as private businesses. Instead, decisions about hours, ages, fees, locations, style, and philosophy of the program are made by the families involved.

Moreover, playgroups are inexpensive. The one we belonged to only cost $10 a month. The parents take turns supervising the group; so there is no outlay for a teacher's salary. Most of the toys, equipment and supplies can be made, scrounged or donated. The cost of rent is low, or nothing at all if the group meets in members' homes. Thus, playgroups can provide convenient, workable, inexpensive childcare for parents.

The playgroup is a good situation for the kids as well. It provides them with playmates. Parents who

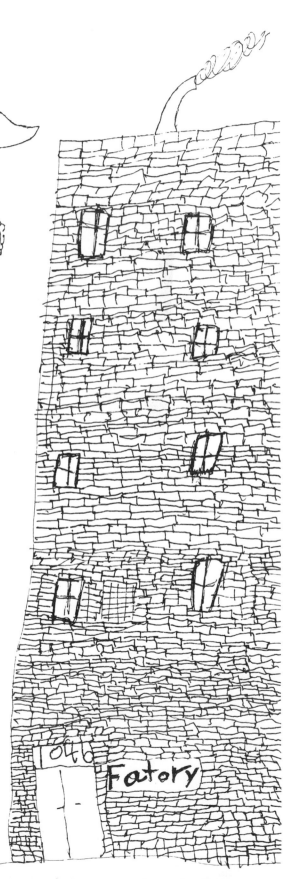

pool their energy and resources can make a more exciting day for kids. Trips to the zoo, the fire station, a factory, the garbage dump, museums, puppet shows, and such—playgroups can give kids many new experiences, more than any individual family could ever provide.

My family belonged to a group that called themselves The Dirty Feet Playgroup (when we felt like having a name). There were all different kinds of families in our group. Some of us didn't have much money and some of us had rather a lot. Some of us had dark skin; some had light skin. Some of us worked nine-to-five jobs; others went to school or worked part-time, and some worked twenty-four hours a day. There were single-parent and double-parent families. We all needed childcare. We had the good fortune to come across each other and work out a way to serve our common needs.

We had fun, too. We launched The Great Balloon Race, built ant farms, grew 10-foot high sunflowers, marveled at dinosaur bones, flew kites, peered through microscopes, made movies, picnicked in the park, created creations of all sorts, toured factories, laid in the sun, yelled at each other, laughed together and generally had a good time. We hope you do, too.

Planning a Playgroup

Playgroups can take many different forms, depending on the needs and circumstances of the parents and kids involved. It would be impossible to list all the different ways that groups can be organized, but these thumbnail sketches should give you some ideas and help you in making your plans.

Playgroup #1 This group involves four families with four children, ages 6-18 months. The playgroup meets four days a week, from nine to noon, in the homes of the members. The fathers all work during the day; so it is the mothers who run the playgroup. One morning a week each mother cares for all the children. On her 'day,' each mother covers the cost of food and diapers. Every other Friday the mothers all meet together to discuss the playgroup and enjoy each other's company.

After operating on this schedule for several months, they decide to schedule the playgroup so that each mother has the group in her home for a week at a time. This way, the parents are able to rearrange furniture and objects to 'childproof' their homes. One family even builds a large communal playpen that is raised off the floor so that children can be reached without a lot of bending and are almost on eye level with the adults.

The new schedule and arrangements also allow the now older and more active group more freedom. As the children get older, the parents all contribute to the purchase of some toys and other play materials that they can transport from house to house in a couple of old suitcases.

The situation works very well and the parents find themselves developing an informal babysitting co-op in the evenings. Each couple is able to spend time together knowing that their children are well cared for in familiar surroundings. Basically, these families have built an extended family situation for themselves. The mothers are delighted with the free time, even though many times they do the same household chores that they would have done if their children had been at home. These women find that having time away from the kids has helped them enjoy and appreciate their kids more fully. The kids, too, develop a new air of independence. The mothers are also pleased because the playgroup has provided at least a partial cure for their 'kid fever'—a common affliction among women who are isolated at home with kids, diapers, and housework. It has also given them the opportunity to discuss their problems and concerns with other women.

Playgroup #2

This group involves six families with seven kids ages 3-5. The playgroup meets five days a week from 9 to 4. One of the families consists of a working father and his daughter. Since he arrives home from work later, arrangements are made for his daughter to come home with another member's children.

Although some of the fathers have time during the day to participate in running the playgroup, as a rule, they don't. Again, it is the mothers who assume the responsibility.

Most of the kids involved in this group have known each other for some time and are unusually cooperative. The mothers decide that it might be possible for one mother to supervise this particular group, provided they have the right physical set-up.

During the planning stages, one of the families moves into an old house that has a small ramshackle cottage behind it with an adjacent area that can be fenced off to make a play yard. The parents patch holes, rewire, tear up rotting floor boards, shoo out the mice, and apply a fresh coat of lead-free paint. After the cost of repairs is deducted, it is agreed that they will pay $60 a month rent.

Five of the mothers take turns being at the 'school,' as they have come to call it, one day a week. The children bring their own lunches and the mother-of-the-day provides a snack. Each day the mother in charge records the day's activities and comments on each child's progress or problems in a log. She might also mention any projects that could be continued the next day. That way each mother knows what the kids have been doing and is able to help them carry through on their projects. The log also enables the mothers to keep in touch with what's happening between meetings.

For the first month the parents meet weekly, but as schedules and routines are ironed out, they begin to meet on a monthly basis. At these meetings they arrange schedules, discuss problems, and plan trips and activities. Each mother presents the activities she has in mind for her days and enlists the help of the other mothers in carrying out her plans.

The working father contributes $60 a month to the playgroup, which is about 1/2 of what he was paying for childcare. The other families pay $10 a month into the kitty. One of the families has a limited income; so they sometimes "work off" their contribution by building equipment or making supplies. The group usually has an income of $110 a month and expenses of only $80. Most of the equipment and toys have been scrounged, made, or donated, so the group is able to run a very nice program on $30 a month and a lot of ingenuity.

Although the group is a very mixed one, in terms of race, income, and lifestyles, they function very well, with a respect for differences. Here again the playgroup set-up has been a success for both parents and kids. Many of the children in this group have no brothers or sisters, and no playmates in their immediate neighborhood. At home they were often lonely and bored and, consequently, made large demands on their parents. The playgroup has provided playmates and a more stimulating environment, so there is no longer the constant demand for parental attention. The parents and kids find that although they are spending less time together, they enjoy the time that they do share more and look forward to being with each other. The parents are also pleased that the children seem to be learning; some of them have even begun to read. One of the mothers is able to return to school, an option she could not have afforded if it weren't for free childcare. Another of the women is able to take a part time job which, although it doesn't pay well, is very satisfying.

This group involves eight families with ten kids, ages 2-5. The group meets from 9-5, five days a week in a converted storefront. Both mothers and fathers work at the storefront. Two of the families have working parents who are unable to be with the group during the day.

Playgroup #3

Each day there are at least two adults in the storefront to supervise the kids. This group decides how many days a week each parent is scheduled to work on the basis of how many parents and kids are in the family. In a single parent family with one kid, for instance, that parent works only half as much as a two-parent family with only one child. On special occasions and field trips some parents help out even though it is not required of them.

Each of the six families who work in the storefront during the day pay between $10 and $25 a month. One of the working parent families pays $35, while the other family, which has a higher income, pays $75 a month. The group's total income is $240 a month. Their expenses for rent on the storefront and utilities comes to $160 a month. The extra money is spent on supplies, toys, and equipment. Again, many of the play materials are made or donated; so the extra money is sufficient to run an exciting program. In fact, after several months of operation, they find that they are able to keep over a month's reserve in their treasury in case some of their income drops off.

In addition to working with the children during the day, each parent belongs to one of several committees—financial, maintenance, equipment, supplies, scheduling, etc. The committees meet as often as necessary. One evening a month the group meets at one member's home to straighten out problems, hear the reports, needs and ideas of the different committees, and to plan programs for the children. That evening, two of the parents care for the children at the storefront during the meeting.

The fact that this playgroup has fathers who are actively involved in the day-to-day care of the kids has had special benefits. The kids who don't live with their fathers have a caring male figure to relate to. Seeing men changing diapers, doing dishes, wiping noses, etc., helps free all the kids from the traditional sex-role stereotypes. The fathers themselves find that they enjoy the opportunity to play a larger part in their kids' lives. For some of the parents, the man's sharing of childcare responsibilities has been a turning point in their relationship and has brought them closer together.

After almost a year of successful operation, despite a few changes in membership, the group finds itself in trouble. They had been using a park for outdoor play space, but for convenience they have recently filled in the dirt parking lot behind their storefront with sand and built some outdoor play equipment. This has attracted attention in the neighborhood. They fear they will be reported and forced to close down because they are unlicensed. The group is determined to fight for what they feel is a safe, inexpensive and healthy childcare program. Committees are formed to do some research, contact state and local politicians who might be sympathetic, and defend themselves against possible problems.

Playgroup #4   Just so you don't think it's all a rose garden, let's look at a less successful playgroup. This playgroup is started by ten families with twelve kids, ages 6 months to 5 years. They rent a single-story house in a location convenient to all. For two months they have planning meetings and work hard getting the house ready.

After only three weeks of operation, there is a lot of tension. Two families are very lax about arriving on time to pick up their children, on one occasion keeping the other parents waiting at the center for several hours. Another parent habitually "forgets" his days to work at the center, leaving the center understaffed.

People constantly make commitments to build toys and equipment which they do not fulfill. In addition, two of the children are real terrors and most of the day is spent trying to deal with the havoc they create with the other children. One parent drops his child off with a temperature and what turns out to be a case of strep throat. The infection spreads, and the center has to close down for a few days, much to the inconvenience of the working parents who depend on the playgroup for childcare while they are working.

Emergency meetings are held. Two of the families are asked to shape up or ship out. Schedules are rearranged so that more adults will be there to supervise the children. Schemes are devised to deal with the difficult children. Things limp along for awhile. But a couple of families with infants drop out because they don't feel their children are receiving proper attention and the infants' naps are continually interrupted by noise from the older children.

One winter morning the parents and children arrive to find that the gas and electricity have been turned off because no one has paid the bills. As a crowning touch, the landlord appears that day saying that the lady next door is complaining about the noise, and the man across the street can't find a place to park his car when he gets home from work. So . . . "you'll have to move, and by the way who gave you permission to paint elephants and giraffes on the wall?" The landlord is taking the people who signed the lease to small claims court. The group has quickly disbanded, leaving everyone with lots of hard feelings.

These four thumbnail sketches should give you an idea of the different ways in which a playgroup can work (or not work, as in the last case). The needs of the members and the resources available will determine what kind of program your group organizes.

Finding People

Getting the right group of people together to form a playgroup has a lot to do with the success of your efforts. First of all, do you like the other people involved? Let's face it, we all meet people from time to time that we simply do not like. If you find that you take an instant dislike to some of the parents or kids involved in your initial meetings, then you may want to regroup and try again. It is also important that the people involved are dependable and reliable. If in the course of your early meetings you find that some people are always late, don't take care of their share of the business, and don't seem willing to change, get rid of them. This may sound a little cold, but people who habitually fail to meet their responsibilities can ruin it for everyone else.

In getting the right group together, you might ask yourself some of these questions. How do the parents involved relate to children? Are they warm and responsive? Do they have enough patience to deal with a group of young children? Are their expectations and treatment of children the same for boys and girls? How do the other parents reward or discipline children? Do you feel comfortable with these methods? How do they deal with potentially explosive situations such as fights over toys or physical aggressiveness?

Don't be misled by differences in people's child-rearing philosophies or life styles. I've found that playgroups where the parents are all of the same political persuasions, lifestyles and philosophies seem to have more trouble than groups with a greater diversity. I'm not sure why there is usually more argument and tension in such groups, perhaps people with similar lifestyles tend to compete to see whose is the more authentic. At any rate, tolerance is an important key to being able to function. Many people are uncertain about their child-rearing methods or are, at least, open to discussion and change. Many of the differences in attitudes can be resolved.

Methods of discipline often vary widely. For instance, in the playgroup we belong to, two of the families occasionally use spanking to discipline their children. It is not my style, but as long as it doesn't go on within the playgroup, it's not really any of my business. If you are a feminist and one of the parents dresses her little girl in organdy frills or ridicules a little boy who plays with a doll, then you've got a problem. Many of these things can be talked over and do not necessarily mean that you cannot work with such people.

There are a number of ways to go about finding people interested in starting playgroups. Don't be discouraged if one method doesn't bring results, keep trying. Remember, there are lots of people out there who need childcare, it's just a matter of getting in touch with each other.

• *Friends, Neighbors* — It is probably best to get started with people you already know. Talking frankly and candidly is easier with a group of friends or acquaintances than with a group of strangers. Even if you only find one or two other families through personal contacts, you can begin to make plans while you are looking for other people. Your starter group can begin to share the work and responsibilities so the group does not come to depend on one person. The more concrete your plans are, the easier it will be to attract other families, even if those plans are eventually altered by the needs of the newcomers.

• *Word of Mouth Network* — Tell friends and acquaintances about your plans and ask them to suggest other people and pass the word on. Childless friends may also be able to help. Good news travels fast.

• *Put up notices* in local grocery stores, laundromats, libraries, parks, etc. Explain that you want to start a playgroup or childcare cooperative. You may also want to explain what you are talking about since some people will not be familiar with the terms. If you have definite ideas about ages, or hours in mind, mention them. If you plan to include working parents, say something about this since many working parents automatically assume that they cannot participate in cooperative childcare ventures. Invite people to call you and talk about the idea.

• *Try calling women's groups* in your area and explain what you are doing. They may be able to put you in touch with other people who are interested or even with folks who are already running playgroups. Their experiences can be encouraging.

• *If there are food co-ops* or other cooperative ventures in your area, get in touch with them. People who have experience working in group efforts will be valuable members of a playgroup.

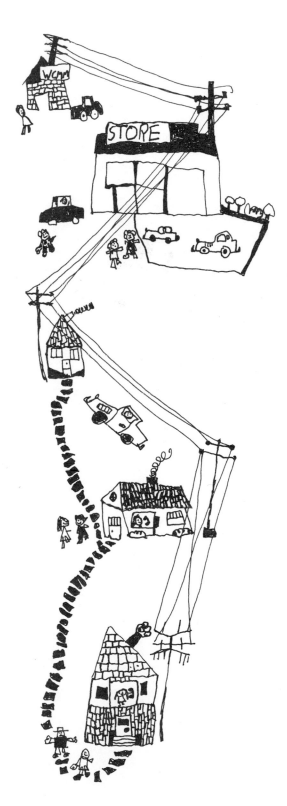

• *Contact public and private pre-schools* in your area. They may be willing to refer people on their waiting list to you.

• *The elementary schools* in your area may also be able to give your name to people interested in child-care.

• *If there are parks* in your neighborhood, there are inevitably lots of mothers and kids hanging around. Try talking over your idea with some of these women.

• *If your local library has a children's section,* talk to the librarian. Such people often have contacts with parents of young children.

• *Sometimes local papers will run ads* for free or for a small cost. Local radio stations may have public service announcements.

As people contact you, keep a list of their names, addresses, phone numbers, ages of children and their child care needs. If more people than you need have responded, you may want to create smaller groups based on the age of children, where they live or the kinds of child care they need. Put those people in touch with each other and start another ball rolling. It is a good idea to keep in touch with any splinter groups. You may be able to help each other as problems arise.

Taking Care of Business

However you manage to get your group together, you will eventually have to sit down together and make some basic decisions. Some of these decisions may have been made in part by the person or people who have been the organizing force, but here is a brief list of some of the basic decisions your group will have to consider.

Ages

What are the age ranges in your group? A group with three infants and a four year old is going to have some problems. Each child should have at least one playmate around his own age. If you are still looking for more members, what ages will you accept?

Size of Group

How many kids do you want in your playgroup? This may be decided by the sites available to you. If you are planning a playgroup that meets in the members' homes, this will probably limit the number of children. Keeping the group fairly small, at least to start, is probably best.

Adult/Kid Ratio

What will be the ratio of parents to kids during the playgroup day? This will depend on the particular parents and the temperament and age of the kids. It is best to start out with a fairly high ratio. You can always cut back later on. If you have infants you will need more people since the infants require more time for feeding, diaper changing and cuddling. A ratio of 1:3 for infants is a safe one, 1:5 is the standard ratio for children three to four years old; for six year olds the recommendation is usually about 1:7. I know of one group where the ratio is 1:8, but many of the parents in this group have had experience working with groups of kids, the kids are of the easy-to-live-with variety, and their physical set-up (small fenced play yard adjacent to the place where the group meets) makes it easy for one parent to supervise the group.

Hours

How often will your playgroup meet—every day? Two or three times a week? For how long—full days? Half days? If working parents are involved, how can you provide full-time childcare for them? Can one member agree to care for the children of working parents before and/or after playgroup? Should this member be paid for this service?

Schedules

How will you decide how much time each family 'owes'? Do families with more than one child owe more time or money? Some groups think of families as belonging to the playgroup; so folks are not penalized for having more than one kid. Do single-parent families owe as much time as families with two parents? Besides the work of actually caring for the kids there are other jobs that working parents may be able to do—maintenance, gathering supplies, building equipment, handling finances, organizing meetings, scheduling, etc. It's a good idea to set your schedule up well in advance so that everyone can make plans accordingly.

Be prepared to deal with the fact that the schedule will be changed a lot. Our group rarely went through a week without some kind of change or substitution, but despite all the rearranging, we always managed to carry on. We began by scheduling two parents each day, but later we found that one parent could handle the group quite nicely. A larger playgroup that we visited scheduled two parents in the mornings and a third parent came at lunch time to help out with the food preparation and afternoon activities. Another playgroup hired a neighborhood teenager who came after school and during the summer. The teenager was delighted with the extra money and the parents were glad to have the help. Still another group had a 'grandmother,' a senior citizen who came a few times a week and read stories or simply held a child in her lap. She refused to take any money for her services, but the group 'paid' her by driving her to the grocery store, doctor's appointments, and such, saving her many long and tiring bus rides. Look around your community for people who might be able to help run your playgroup.

Men

It is often difficult to find families with fathers who can take part in the actual day-to-day running of the playgroup. Many men have jobs that require them to be at work during the playgroup hours. Even those who have different schedules or more flexible hours may be too macho to participate in 'woman's work' of caring for children. But it's worth it to hunt around for men who would be willing and able to spend time with the kids. A caring male figure is especially important to kids who have no father in their own home. Being around men who are operating outside the traditional male role is a healthy experience for all the kids—and for the adults as well. One playgroup decided that having the men participate was so important that they organized their playgroup so that it met on Saturdays as well, which gave all the fathers a chance to participate.

If your group is going to meet in the homes of members, does everyone have enough space to accommodate the kids? How will you rotate—each day, by the week? If you plan to rent space, there may be some difficulties. Who will sign the lease? The group must agree beforehand to share the financial responsibility of the lease if the playgroup does not work out. If there is no lease, are you willing to take the risk of being evicted? If you rent space, make sure the landlord understands what you are doing. It is also a good idea to check out the neighbors and find out how they feel about your being there and how you can work out any inconvenience you might cause them.

Finding a suitable site is a big task, but if you keep your eyes open it is not too difficult.

*A large garage or basement in one of the members' homes can be fixed up to accommodate a playgroup.

*Churches or community centers may have some space that you can use. Often such space will be shared, used by other groups in the evenings or on weekends. There is some inconvenience in such an arrangement since you often have to pack up the whole (school) each week or even each day, but many groups function very well under shared-space arrangements.

*Store fronts or office space in some sections of town may be very inexpensive. There is often a parking space in the rear that can be converted into a playground. Look for empty store fronts on side streets. Remember that an unlicensed group may have to maintain a low profile.

*Houses or Apartments — Renting a house or apartment can be difficult because of the lease and neighbor problem. However, many landlords will be pleased to rent to a group that is willing to do some repair work.

If you are operating out of members' homes, money may not be too much of a problem. There may not even be any money involved; the parents may simply pay the costs of their day. Or, each family could pay a small fee each month to cover the costs of food, activities, toys or trips.

If you are renting space you will need to consider the costs of rent, utilities, phone, supplies, equipment, toys and any extra help. Unless the children bring lunches and their own snacks, you may need to include food in your budget. You might need some

Site

When looking for space, keep these things in mind:

*Is it conveniently located?

*Is it large enough? The standard recommendation is 35 square feet of indoor playspace and 75 square feet of outdoor playspace for each child.

*Does it have a sink and toilet; do they work?

*How is the place heated? Is the heating adequate? Is the system vented, safe?

*Does it have enough light?

*Is there outdoor playspace that can be fenced off or is there a park nearby?

*Is the landlord sympathetic, are the neighbors likely to be inconvenienced?

*There should be at least two exits in case of fire.

*Is the electrical wiring safe, are there enough electrical outlets to support enough light, a phonograph, etc.

*Are there hazardous steps, lead-based paint?

*How much time/money must be invested to make the space usable? Is the landlord agreeable to your renovation plans?

Budget

initial money to pay for phone installation, equipment, repairs and painting. You may also have to pay a deposit or cleaning fee on rented space. Most of your toys, equipment and materials can be donated, scrounged, found or made by the group.

Your income will have to cover your basic expenses. Each family can contribute to the kitty. Will it be a flat rate per kid or per family or will the fee be on a sliding scale, based on ability to pay? Working parents may be able to pay a fair amount to the playgroup and still pay less than the standard fee for child care. In such cases both the working parent families and the other families can benefit. Even if you have to pay a fairly high rent, you will find that the cost of a playgroup is much lower than any other form of childcare.

It is a good idea to have one person handling the money and paying the bills, so that confusion doesn't set in. The playgroup we belonged to cost ten dollars a month and one day a week working at the center, which was not a bad deal for full-time, five-day-a-week childcare. Sometimes a family had trouble even with this small amount and it was understood that if someone didn't have the cash to pay that was okay, too. Because we operated on such a small budget almost all the equipment was donated or made by the parents. Having gotten into the habit of being ingenious (or stingy), we found that we usually had a surplus in our budget that we never seemed to spend.

Legalities   It's a good idea to assign one or two people to the task of investigating the legal aspects of your playgroup.

The first area you should check into is licensing. Most states have some sort of laws regulating child care programs. Usually, these laws are administered by the welfare or health department, or, less frequently, the education department. These departments grant a license that allows qualified individuals or groups to run a childcare program. In some states, small, informal, parent-run programs like playgroups do not need a license. Other states will require a license. In still other states, the laws are written in a way that makes playgroups illegal. In California, for instance, the law requires that all childcare programs, even parent-run cooperatives, have a licensed Early Childhood Education teacher. The teacher's salary alone would make the cost of running a playgroup prohibitive for many people.

10

On one hand, the licensing laws seem just and reasonable, designed to protect parents and children from ignorant or unscrupulous people who might create an overcrowded, unsafe, poorly supervised or unsanitary program. To protect the public, licensing agenices have a number of rules and regulations. For example, the agency might specify a certain amount of indoor and outdoor play space per child, a minimum adult/child ratio, a site free of safety hazards, proper emergency/fire exits, and other health or safety regulations.

On the other hand, it seems a gross infringement of individual rights to prevent parents from getting together and sharing childcare. We would not allow the state to require that an individual family with eight kids hire a teacher to help them raise their children. Why, then, do we allow the state to make this requirement of a group of families with eight kids who want to share childcare? A government that required its citizens to raise their children in communal childcare situations would be a totalitarian monstrosity, stripping its citizens of a basic freedom of choice. Yet, the effect of the laws in some states is that parents are required to raise children within the confines of a nuclear family. (Unless of course, they have enough money to pay for childcare, in which case you can buy your freedom of choice).

Obviously, the laws governing childcare need to be revised in many states. Perhaps licensing agencies could distinguish between large profit-making or industry/government funded programs and small, parent-run, neighborhood playgroups. Agencies could adopt a new attitude toward parent-run programs. Instead of being watchdogs, they could lend their expertise to help parents start badly needed programs and to make sure that parents don't create dangerous programs out of ignorance.

Until this happens, parents will continue to organize their own alternatives, regardless of the laws. In many cases licensing agencies are small and understaffed. Non-profit parent-run groups are not likely to come under the scrutiny of public agencies unless a specific complaint is made. Although I do not know of playgroups that have actually been prosecuted for violation of childcare laws, I do know of groups that have been forced to close down. The usual procedure in my state is for the state agency to issue a warning to any unlicensed group that they discover. If the group does not heed the warning and comply with licensing regulations, they are forced to close down or face prosecution.

Check out the laws governing childcare in your state by calling the appropriate agencies. You may not have to deal with the licensing hassle at all. If, however, you discover that your state has prohibitive licensing laws, everyone in the group should know exactly what risks and penalties are involved.

There are also other legal considerations. If the members are meeting in each others' homes and a child is injured on the premises those parents could be legally liable. Sometimes an inexpensive home-owner's policy will cover this. For licensed groups it is sometimes possible to purchase a special insurance that will cover each child for about $1 a year. The licensing agency will provide this information. It is best that the parents involved discuss these problems beforehand so there are no misunderstandings later on. There is sometimes no way to protect yourself legally in an unlicensed playgroup, so there must be an atmosphere of trust between the families involved.

Emergency Procedures

Before you begin operation it is important that everyone be aware of emergency procedures. Everyone should know what to do in case of fire, how to operate an extinguisher, what to do in event of an earthquake, flood, famine, etc. One person should be responsible for devising emergency procedures. Many licensing agencies will require a group to provide an "emergency evacuation plan," which is simply a plan of how to get the kids to safety in case of disaster (fire or the building collapsing, etc.). It helps to know ahead of time that if a fire starts in the front of the building, parent #1 is going to check the bathroom and kitchen for kids, while parent #2 will get the kids in the main playroom out. Of course, disaster never strikes according to plan, but if you've at least considered the problems and procedures beforehand, you have a better chance of surviving.

The parents should know about any special medical problems the children may have, for instance, food or drug allergies. Each parent should also be aware of basic first aid procedures—how to treat a burn, convulsions, electric shock, spinal injuries, broken arm, etc. If one of the parents has some first aid training, they should devote some time to educating the other parents. Groups like the Red Cross will give first aid training, and their first-aid manual is a good source book on emergency treatment. The parents should also know how to give mouth-to-mouth resuscitation (which is a somewhat different technique for children than it is for adults). Of course, the group should have a well stocked first aid kit available at all times.

Next to the phone you should keep a list of phone numbers of fire station, police, ambulance, rescue squad, and places where parents can be reached in case of emergency. The names and numbers of family doctors and nearest emergency hospital should be on the list as well. All the parents should fill out emergency treatment release forms. This form will allow the parent(s) in charge of the group to authorize treatment in case the parents cannot be reached. Each parent should fill out one form and give it to their family doctor or medical plan and another form should be filed at the nearest emergency hospital. We also keep a form for each child in the first aid kit. Luckily, we never had occasion to use any of these emergency procedures, but it is foolish not to be prepared.

You should also decide beforehand what your policy on colds and sniffles is going to be. People have amazingly different notions on this subject. I have known some parents who are horrified if another kid shows up with a runny nose for fear their child will catch a cold. Personally, my attitude is a lot more casual and since we pass out vitamin C at playgroup, it's not too much of a problem.

Many of the rules and policies of your playgroup will evolve and change as different situations and problems arise. There are certain things it is a good idea to discuss beforehand. For instance, what is your group's policy on illness? If a child is sick and misses a week of school, does that parent still owe the same amount of time or money to the playgroup? If the parent is unable to be with the playgroup on his/her day, whose responsibility is it to find a substitute? How about discipline: What methods? What are your ground rules here? There may also be certain ground rules associated with the site you have chosen for the playgroup: don't run through the ivy patch, no standing on the orange crate bookshelves, etc. What kind of food is to be provided for snacks and lunches— Hostess Twinkies and Kool-Aid or carrot sticks and apple juice? It is impossible to anticipate all the questions and problems, so it is important that the parents meet on a regular basis to discuss the playgroup and make plans.

AUTHORIZATION TO CONSENT TO
TREATMENT OF MINOR

(I)(We, the undersigned, parent(s) to
a minor, do hereby authorize
as agent(s) for the undersigned to consent to any x-ray examination, anesthetic, medical or surgical diagnosis or treatment and hospital care which is deemed advisable by, and is to be rendered under the general or special supervision of any physician and surgeon licensed under the provisions of the medicine practice act on the medical staff of   hospital, whether such diagnosis or treatment is rendered at the office of said physician or at said hospital.

It is understood that this authorization is given in advance of any specific diagnosis, treatment or hospital care being required, but is given to provide authority and power on the part of our aforesaid agent(s) to give specific consent to any and all such diagnosis, treatment or hospital care which the aforementioned physician in the exercise of his best judgement may deem advisable.

This authorization is given pursuant to the provisions of Section 258 of the Civil Code of California.

This authorization shall remain effective until   19
unless sooner revoked in writing delivered to said agent(s)

Dated

                    Father

Witness   Mother

Witness   Legal Guardian

The Playgroup Day

At some time during your planning meetings your group will have to talk concretely and practically about what the parents and kids are going to do during the playgroup day. Many parents will want "something more than babysitting." Others may have vague educational goals: "I want my child to learn something." For some parents this may mean some kind of beginning reading or math activities or exposure to "educational toys." For other parents this may mean an exciting environment where children are free to explore and are stimulated to try new things. It requires a good deal of planning to create and maintain an exciting program and environment that will keep kids stimulated. You will have to decide how much preparation is expected of parents who will be supervising the kids. Are they responsible for planning activities and supplying materials? Since the same parents will not be at the center each day you may have a problem in continuity. How will you arrange to follow through on interests and projects that develop?

Whatever kind of program you decide upon, your playgroup should have some fairly consistent daily schedule—a certain time for lunches, snacks, naps. You may have to schedule a specific time for outdoor play if your play area is not immediately adjacent and kids cannot come and go as they please.

Our playgroup made a number of games and toys like the ones described in this book. The kids donated some of their own toys and we managed to scrounge a lot of supplies. We also bought some items with the money we had left over after paying our monthly expenses. We made sure the kids had plenty of play choices. There were arts and crafts supplies, blocks, cars, dolls, dress up clothes, sand box, climbing apparatus, etc. The parents also brought materials for special projects from time to time.

We tried to include some activities that were educational in the academic sense. For instance, all of the kids had their own word boxes which contained cards with words the kids had chosen printed on them. Oftentimes we would use the word boxes at 'quiet time.' We would spend a few minutes with each of the kids who was not napping, going through their boxes and adding new words. Even though most of the kids did not read, they enjoyed the process of choosing words, getting a bit of one-to-one attention and, of course, decorating the words appropriately. Some of the younger kids got interested in the alphabet and used their word boxes to learn letter names and sounds.

Since our parent meetings were held only once a month, we needed some way of keeping in touch; so we decided to keep a log. Each parent recorded the day's activities briefly so the other parents could tell at a glance what the kids had been doing. If they got involved in an activity that needed to be followed through, this was mentioned in the log. For instance, one day the kids got involved in making a submarine out of a discarded water heater box. They carefully removed the exposed staples with pliers and painted their submarine lavishly. There was no time to finish the painting and cut the windows they had planned that day. The project was recorded in the log so the parents and kids could continue the project on the next day. Sometimes one parent would call another, asking that special materials be brought to finish a project. With the submarine project, the kids got to talking on the way home about how the submarine should have "one of those tubes sticking out of it" (a periscope). That night the mother called the parents who were going to have the group the next day to arrange for a couple of mirrors and a large tube to make the necessary periscope.

At the parent meetings, each parent suggested projects and activities they had in mind, outlining the costs and enlisting the other parents' help. For example, one parent decided to keep a chart of the moon's phases. She asked the other parents and kids to look at the moon every night. In the mornings one

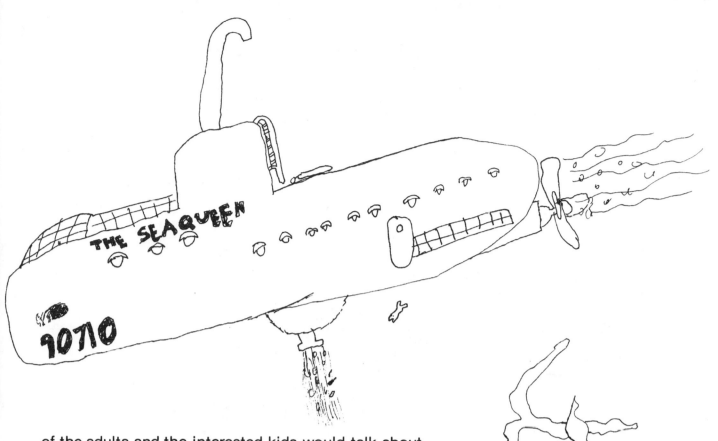

of the adults and the interested kids would talk about how the moon looked and draw the appropriate symbol on the chart. Many times one of the parents would ask the kids for suggestions about what they would like to do and would bring their ideas to the monthly parent meetings.

Although the parents usually came to playgroup with some plans in mind, many times the plans would not be used that day. If the kids were already involved in another project from the day before or had devised some project of their own, this usually took precedence over the plans of the parents. Many times projects and activities developed spontaneously as the parents and kids worked and played together during the day.

There is a fine balance between planned and unplanned activities. It is important that the kids aren't bored, but there should be plenty of time for plain old-fashioned play. If the kids are fighting and squabbling a lot they are probably pretty bored. You may want to plan more activities or enrich your environment. On the other hand, too much stimulus can be confusing. Over-planning or over-direction can lead to "Aw, do I have to?" or "No, I don't want to." Experience will help you find the proper balance. Hopefully, the ideas in the rest of this book will help you plan an exciting playgroup.

Making Kidspace

How you organize your space, whether it's in a home, shared space or rented space, has a big effect on how smoothly your playgroup operates. It's best to organize your space cafeteria-style, with a number of different interest areas so that kids can select from a variety of play opportunities. This way each kid or group of kids is free to pursue their own interests and adults don't get stuck trying to discipline everyone into a single group activity. Ideally your space should include areas like these:

Puzzles, Games, Manipulatives

There should be an area for storage of games, puzzles, "educational toys," math and reading aids, magnets, magnifying glasses, etc. There should be some place for the kids to play with these materials away from the noisier goings on.

Housekeeping

Playing house is also a popular fantasy. Kids will enjoy a corner with some orange-crate stoves, refrigerators, sinks, and dolls, cribs, carriages. One group decided to place their housekeeping corner up up in a loft so that some of the more passive girls in the group would be encouraged to climb and the boys would be included in the housekeeping play despite what they had already learned about their male role. Or, instead of a housekeeping area, you might make a pretend store, post office, etc.

Kids really get into acting out their fantasies. A corner with a trunk full of old clothes, hats, puppets and a puppet theatre, masks, a dollhouse, etc., will keep kids occupied for hours. If possible, include a large mirror, so that kids can admire their finery. A shoebox full of theatrical makeup is a messy but delightful addition. If your kids get into drama, you might rig up a curtain that could define a stage for spontaneous theatrical productions.

Drama

Music   Because space is usually limited it's sometimes hard to make an ideal music area—one that is far enough from the noisier play areas. Such an area could include a record player simple enough for children to operate and a selection of records. Some of the cassette tape recorders will take the place of a record player and some have the additional advantage of being able to record. The area could also include rhythm band and other musical instruments. Sometimes it is possible to fix up a recorder or record player with ear phones so that the music or stories can be listened to without interrupting others. If you can't scrounge or afford a set of earphones, try simple ear plugs that only cost a couple of bucks.

Arts & Crafts   There should be an area with a child-sized table which can be as simple as a plank of plywood painted with enamel or covered with contact paper so the surface is washable. It can be propped up with orange crates and taken down and stored easily. There should be the usual paints, crayons, paper, scissors, glue, paste, clay, etc., available for the kids. Adults can save themselves a lot of extra steps if they organize the supplies so that the kids can set up and clean up by themselves. If you are cramped for space it is possible to make small movable desks out of tri-wall cardboard or mailing tubes, that can be taken apart and stored easily.

This area could include a box of scrap wood, some well-made child-sized tools, and a carpentry bench with clamps or vises to hold the wood while kids hammer and saw. You might have to store the tools out of reach so the children can only use them with supervision.

Carpentry

As quiet as possible, away from the louder activities. Fill it with books, comfortable chairs, beanbags, or cushions. Many times a loft, enclosed or covered with curtains, will increase floor space and provide a quiet refuge. A portion of the room covered with a rug and cushions can be sectioned off with curtains or room dividers. If you are operating out of members' homes, it is usually possible to find a nook for a library. One enterprising family with a large old-fashioned bathroom has a library in the corner opposite the bathtub.

Reading

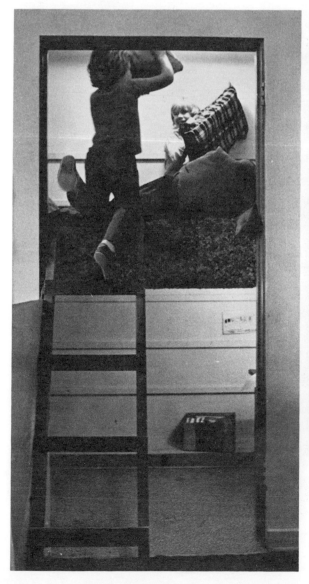

Private Spaces   It's a nice idea for everyone to have their own private space for storing treasures. Cubbyholes can be made out of stacked boxes, crates or mailing tubes. If your space permits, you should include some areas designed for privacy. This may be as simple as some fiberboard drums or large appliance boxes with doors cut in them, set in a quiet corner.

Blocks   This area should be large enough to allow great, sprawling constructions to develop without interference. It should include a large-sized set of blocks and some block storage arrangement. Trucks, cars, wooden people and animals are a nice addition to this area.

If you have the space, these activities can go on outside, otherwise, it is possible to construct sand and water tables, that can be used indoors, out of wood or tri-wall cardboard lined with plastic. Smocks made out of heavy-duty garbage bags or old raincoats will keep kids dry as they play.

Sand & Water

If you have an outdoor space this area should include equipment for exercising those big muscles. See Adventure Playgrounds (page 80).

Active Play

Of course, this is an ideal situation and your group will have to work within the limitations of the space available to you. Many of these areas will overlap. In small spaces or shared space, you can rely on portable furniture made out of tri-wall cardboard that can be taken down and stored. You can increase floor space in a home by building a "murphy" bed that folds up into the wall. (Beds take up an inordinate amount of wasted space anyhow!) Lofts are another way of increasing floor space and, of course, it is important that they be sturdily constructed. Carrels like the one pictured below can increase floor space, and provide work areas and private space.

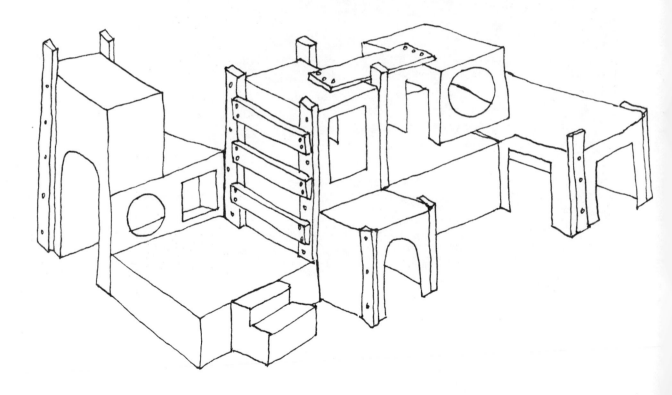

The following list of books will help you in your design efforts:

Farallones Scrapbook: Making Places, Changing Spaces, in Schools, at Home, and Within Ourselves, done by a group of people called Farallones. It's distributed by Random House. It's a real treasure of a book that includes information on building carrels, space dividers, cardboard carpentry, inflatables. A good book for teachers who want to reshape their classroom environment and for playgroups that have rented space in which they are free to build.

Pre-school Equipment. This booklet is particularly valuable to groups who are sharing space in a community center, church or whatever. It has detailed instructions for building sturdy, practical, fun equipment that can be taken apart and stored easily. The booklet is prepared by Stone Mountain Educational Projects Incorporated, a group of former Headstart workers. The booklet costs $2 and is available by writing to Stone Mountain, Roaring Brook Farm, Conway, MA 01341. They also publish another booklet called *Children's Things,* which costs $4 and has 64 pages of instructions for making inexpensive play equipment for preschool programs.

Building with Tires, Building with Tubes, Building with Cardboard. These three booklets are available from the Advisory for Open Education, 55 Chapel Street, Newton, MA 02160. Write and ask for their list of publications and prices. They also publish a number of other goodies. These books are particularly good because they include detailed instructions on how to work with the different materials as well as specific designs. Groups that need to have lightweight portable equipment will find lots of designs for pop-together desks, chairs, bookcases, storage areas, tables, etc.

Cardboard Carpentry Workshop, The Further Adventures of Cardboard Carpentry. These booklets are available from the Workshop for Learning Things, Inc., 5 Bridge Street, Newton, MA. Send 50¢ for a copy of their informative catalog. In addition to these books, they sell cardboard carpentry tools, books, printing materials and a whole wealth of wonderful learning things. I buy the catalog every year just to see what new wonders they've come up with.

Just as a reminder, try to scale your environment to a child's size. I am constantly amazed to find pre-school programs that have spent lots of money on such incongruous pieces of equipment as a four-foot high work table, heavy wooden chairs too cumbersome for children to move, or a teacher's desk.

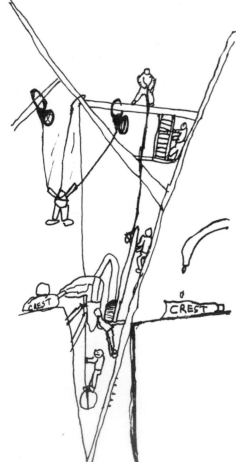

Imagine for a moment that you live in a world run by giants two or three times your size. These giants are incredibly more agile and stronger than you are. Of course, this world is designed for the comfort and convenience of these giants. You are a virtual prisoner of whatever room you find yourself in because the doors are so heavy and the handles too high for you to reach. The simple act of getting yourself a glass of water is full of insurmountable difficulties. The faucets on the sink are too high for you to reach and they may be too tight for your smaller, weaker hands to operate. The glasses may be too wide for your small hands to hold. You may succeed in climbing to the great heights. Balanced precariously, you may be able to fill your glass if the faucets are loose enough, but getting down again with your two hands holding the wide glass is impossible. You take the chance of holding the glass in one hand. It slips, falls to the floor, and breaks. To top it off, the giants are furious with you for your clumsiness!

It's difficult to function in a world built for giants. The better job you can do of scaling your playgroup down to child-size, the easier it will be for both parents and kids. The adults won't be called upon to do "step and fetch it" jobs, freeing their time for more

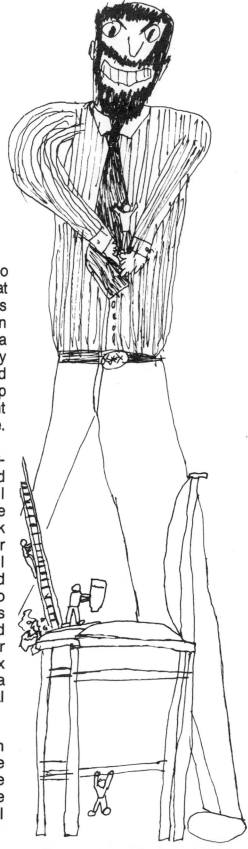

creative interactions. The children will be able to develop the sense of self-confidence and pride that comes from increased self-sufficiency. In some cases this scaling down may be difficult, especially in members' homes. But there are simple things, like a set of child-sized glasses and a few strategically placed wooden boxes to help reach sinks, toilets, and light switches, that can make life easier for all. Keep yourselves tuned to difficulties in your environment and devise remedies for the problems as they arise.

Another important factor in designing your playgroup environment is change. Toys, games, and materials that are used infrequently or not at all should be removed. Many times these things can be stored for a couple of months and then brought back again. Take your cue from the kids about when your environment needs to be reshaped. Their behavior will tell you when things are becoming stale. We found that our playgroup needed major changes every two or three months. At first, we made these changes rather dramatically, adding piles of new supplies and newly devised toys all at once. Later, we made our changes more gradually, adding, say, a make-up box one week, some new dress-up clothes another, a puppet theater a few weeks later. The gradual changes seemed to work better for our group.

As the months went by, we found that in addition to reshaping the environment, we needed to rely more heavily on special projects and activities to keep the kids, especially the older ones, happily occupied. The next section describes some of our more successful projects, activities, and happenings.

Grandiose Schemes

The projects and activities described in this section were done by the adults and kids in our playgroup (plus a few extra friends from time to time). Some of them were rather elaborate undertakings that were spread out over a number of weeks; others were short one-day affairs. Many of the projects were done more than once. We found that some of the projects required a great deal of parent preparation and participation. Others the kids can do pretty much by themselves.

The kids' level of participation depended on their ages, stage of development, and interest in the activity. Many times the younger kids would participate in activities that really made more sense for the older ones, but they still enjoyed being included. Sometimes children would decline to participate in a project and wander off to do something else. Often they

would return to the group after the project was under-way, having decided that it looked like fun after all. Although we would occasionally encourage shy or less confident children to participate, we usually let the kids make their own decisions about what they wanted to do.

The projects described here go beyond the scope of the usual cut-and-paste arts and crafts and ABC learning that go on in most nursery school programs. They are not a curriculum or step by step guide of what to do. They are merely descriptions of what we did. Hopefully, they will start you off in exciting directions. If you decide to try some of these pro-jects, keep yourself tuned to the needs, ideas, and suggestions of your group. You may find that al-though you started to do one of the projects de-scribed here, you will end up doing something entire-ly different. And that's the way it should be.

Photography

Our kids are going to grow up in the land of tomorrow. If today's seers are right, papers, pencils and books will be obsolete. Communication will be verbal and visual in a world linked by a three-dimensional laser beam communication system. People will communicate in a language of images as well as words . . . Perhaps that's getting into the realm of science fiction, but we did pursue some photography and film-making projects that acquainted the kids with the tools of visual communication and expression. At any rate, we had fun.

Skin Photography

The word photograph comes from the Greek words *photos,* which means light, and *graphos,* which means to write. Basically that's what photography is all about—writing with light. To make a simple photograph you need some sort of surface that is sensitive to light and some way of blocking light from that surface. We began our photography projects with a light-sensitive surface that everyone has available—our skin.

When you remove a bandaid, the portion of skin that was covered is, of course, lighter than the tanned areas of your skin that have been exposed to the sunlight. Using this amazing discovery, we "wrote with light" on our skins by taping adhesive to our bodies before we set out for the beach one day. Some of the kids wrote their names in tape on their backs; others made elaborate designs on their bellies. At the end of the day we stripped off the adhesive and delighted in our skin photographs. We looked a bit strange, but we did learn something.

Light & Shadow

To be a good photographer, you need to have a special awareness of light, to perceive its many subtle qualities. If you squint tightly, so that your eyes are almost closed, you will become aware of the different light sources around you. Ask the kids to try this and to identify where the light is coming from. Which centers of light are brightest, dimmest?

Another exercise that heightens awareness of light is peering at objects through a tube. We gave the kids cardboard tubes from rolls of paper towels and asked them to single out different objects in the room, noting how light touched those objects. Are they brighter on one side than the other? Do some objects seem to reflect more light than others? Do they cast shadows?

Where does the light stop and the shadow start? Do the objects look different inside a room than they do out in the sunlight? Questions like these will help kids focus their attention on the quantity and quality of the light around them. You may find that their perceptions are more acute than yours. Their eyes are younger, fresher and do not take as much for granted.

Shadows occur when light is blocked. It is the shadows of the objects that help define and delineate them. Go shadow hunting, picking out some interesting shadows around you. You can save shadows by slipping a piece of paper under the shadow and tracing it. Take your collection of shadows, cut them out, and mount them on colored paper. We also made shadow portraits of each other by taping a piece of white paper to the wall and positioning each other between the paper and a strong light source. Then we traced around the shadows of each other's profiles that were cast on the paper, cut around the tracings, and mounted them on black paper.

Shadows are fleeting things. They change with the light and disappear when there is no light. Playing with flashlights in a darkened room teaches a lot about shadows and how they work. Do the shadows cast by an object change as you move the flashlight around? What happens when you shine the flashlight directly above an object? On the side? From below? One shadow experiment that the kids particularly enjoyed was tracing each others' shadows on the sidewalk with chalk. We began early in the morning. First we each marked an x on the sidewalk. Then we stood on our x while someone traced our shadow. Around noontime we stood on our x's and had our shadows traced again. At the end of the day as the sun was setting we repeated the process. There on the sidewalk we had a graphic illustration of how shadows change with the light.

Photograms

Photograms are another way of recording shadows. To make a photogram you will need a package of studio proof paper, some objects to lay on the paper, a dimly lit room, and a tray of photographic fixer. In the dim light remove a piece of paper from the package and lay it, smooth side up, on a flat surface. Make sure that you have the smooth side up, for that side is coated with silver bromide crystals which grow dark when light strikes them. When you have your objects arranged, you are ready to expose the paper to sunlight. Be careful not to jostle the objects or the outlines of your photogram will be blurred. When the uncovered portions of the paper turn a good dark color, go back inside and remove the objects. Then put the paper between the pages of a book so that no light can touch it. If you were to open the book to get a look at your photogram, you would see white shadows where the objects had prevented light from striking the paper. But you would only be able to enjoy your photogram for a short time. After a while the light would darken those areas as well. If you want to preserve your photogram, you will need to soak it in a solution that photographers call fixer. The fixer will remove the light sensitive crystals from the paper so that they will no longer react to sunlight and your light areas will remain light. It will also turn the purple brown color of the dark areas to a lighter, orange-brown. (See Appendix for information about fixing, washing and drying.)

This photogram was made by a four-year-old using her hand and a daisy. The possibilities for creating photograms are endless. Experiment with different designs, shapes and sizes of objects. Include objects that let some light pass through as well as objects that block out light entirely. Try building up different patterns with successive exposures on the same piece of paper. Vary the light source (a diffused light, indirect sunlight, direct sunlight) or exposure time on a single sheet. We made a game that involved matching objects with photograms. One time each of the kids made photograms of their hands. Afterwards we hung them on the wall and asked parents to pick out their own children's hands.

You can take the photogram one step further and reverse the shadows so that you have dark objects on a light background. What you are doing here is using your original photogram as a paper negative to make a positive print. Doing this will help the children to understand how film negatives are used to make photographs.

To reverse a photogram, take one that's been washed and dried back into a darkened room. Place an unexposed sheet of studio proof paper underneath the photogram so that the coated sides of each sheet are touching each other. Lay a sheet of glass (with its edges taped for safety) on top of the two sheets of paper. Now you are ready to set the sheets and the glass in strong sunlight. The light will not pass through the dark area of your original photogram, so those areas will be lighter in your new photogram. Conversely, the areas that were light in your first photogram will not block the light, and those areas will be dark in your reversed photogram. You will need a longer exposure time for this second photogram. To determine when you have enough exposure, you will have to take a peek. This is a little tricky since you must be careful not to move the paper, or you'll have a double exposure. With a little experimenting, you should get a pretty good feel for when you have had enough sunlight to get the proper light and dark areas. Fix, wash and dry your reversed photogram just as you did your first one.

Once you have made paper negatives, you are ready to experiment with pinhole cameras. I made my first camera when I was eight years old. I was amazed then that it actually worked and I'm still amazed.

If you and your group are planning to build some cameras, you might start out by thinking about how our own built-in, living cameras—our eyes—work. Look in the mirror or at each other's eyes. The black circle that you see is, of course, the pupil. It is actually a hole that lets light into your eyes. You also have an eyelid that moves up and down over the pupil. Thus, it can admit or block light entering the eye. Although you won't be able to see it, your eye also has a lining in the back, behind the pupil, that is sensitive to light and is called the retina. A pinhole camera is simply a crude version of your eye. To make a pinhole camera you will need:
- a box or container of some sort that will be the camera body or "eyeball,"
- a pin to make a small hole or "pupil" in one end of your box,
- a small piece of cardboard to make a flap that will act as the shutter or "eyelid,"
- a light sensitive lining that will act as the retina or film for your camera. We used film with a speed of 125 (the speed of the film refers to how sensitive the film is to light, how fast its coating reacts to sunlight). The film comes in sheets with ten,

Reversed Photograms

Pinhole Cameras

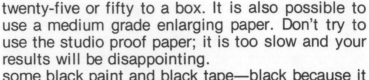

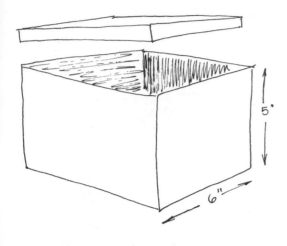

twenty-five or fifty to a box. It is also possible to use a medium grade enlarging paper. Don't try to use the studio proof paper; it is too slow and your results will be disappointing.

- some black paint and black tape—black because it will not reflect stray light rays and send them bouncing around inside your camera.
- two pieces of 5" by 6" cardboard, and some aluminum foil.

The camera described here worked well for us, but almost any size or shape container will do. A shoe box or oatmeal box will do nicely. I have even seen pinhole cameras made from rubber beach balls. Feel free to improvise your own design.

We used a box 6" long and 5" wide that had a removable lid, both of which we painted black on the inside. First, we made a film holder for our film (or paper if that's what you're using). We cut two pieces of cardboard 6" by 5" and painted them black. From one of these pieces we cut a horseshoe-like opening 4-1/16" by 5-1/8" (Fig. A). In the other piece we cut a similar opening 3-5/8" by 4-5/8" (Fig. B).

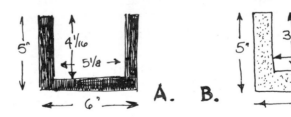

Then we glued the piece with the largest opening (A) to one end of the box with the open end of the horseshoe pointing upward. Then we glued the second piece (B) to the first piece, again with the opening upward, like so:

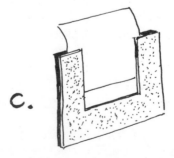

This holder will keep your film or paper in place.

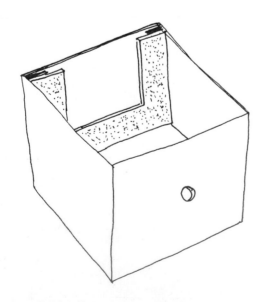

In the center of the other end of the box, directly opposite from the film holder, we cut a hole 1/2" in diameter.

Next, we cut a piece of aluminum foil about 1" square. Laying this flat on a piece of cardboard we used a #10 sewing needle to make a smooth edged hole in the center of the square of foil. The hole should not be too large or it will admit too many light rays and result in a blurred image. Too small a hole will cause the light rays to strike the edges and defract which will produce fuzzy edges on your picture. Your pictures will also be distorted if the hole is not smooth.

Moving right along . . ., we taped the square of foil on the inside of the box right over the 1/2" hole we had cut.

Then we taped a shutter that we made from a small piece of cardboard on the outside of the box covering the hole. We also taped all the outside edges and corners of our box with black tape to avoid light leaks.

Finally we drew a line from the rear corners to the center of the front edge of our camera to make a view-finder. Anything sighted within these lines was also seen by the camera.

At last our cameras were finished and we went back into the dark closet to load them. We took film of the proper size and slipped it into the film holder. Then, we taped the lid on so no light could get in; we were ready to take our first pictures.

If you use film with a speed of about 125 you will need an exposure of about 10 seconds on a bright, sunny day. If the day is cloudy or the light source is weak, you will need more exposure time. With enlarging paper you will need about one minute of exposure time on a bright day.* I prefer film for a pinhole camera simply because most kids won't be able to hold perfectly still for a whole minute. Also, if you use paper, your image will be negative or reversed. To make a positive involves another step, just like making a reversed photogram. It's best to photograph stationary objects with a pinhole camera because any movement by the photographer or the object being photographed will blur the image. You can avoid some of this problem if you set the camera on a table, the ground, a convenient rock, or whatever, while taking the picture.

*Although dim light will not harm studio proof paper, enlarging paper and film must be handled in *complete* darkness.

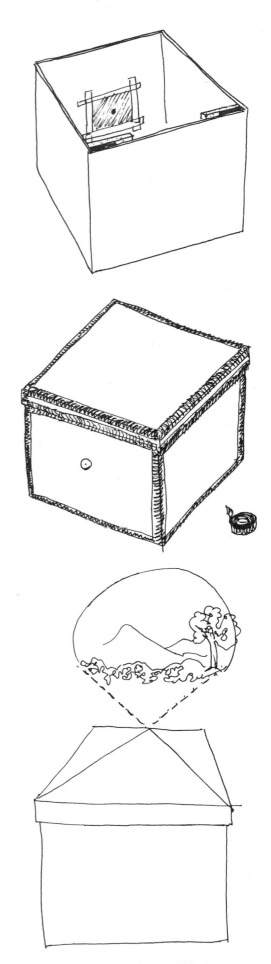

Once you have taken your picture, quickly replace the shutter flap. You must return to the closet or darkroom to remove the film and reload your camera. It is possible to purchase a changing bag which is a two-layered, double-zippered black bag used by photographers. It looks like this:

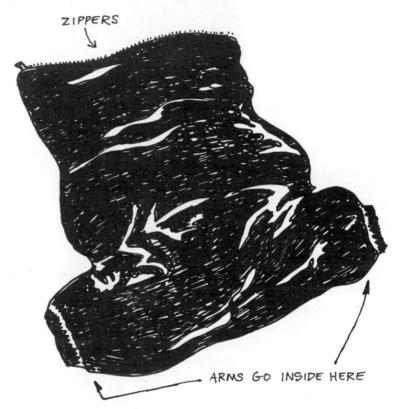

ZIPPERS

ARMS GO INSIDE HERE

You simply unzip the bag, put your camera and unexposed film and a light-tight box inside, zip it up, stick your arms inside and reload your camera, making sure your exposed film is safely inside the box before unzipping.

Since pinhole cameras are so cheap, it's possible to make several so that you won't have to reload all the time. Remember to keep your film and paper in a light-tight place until you are ready to process it. (For developing instructions, see Appendix.)

If you are working with a group of young kids, it might be wise to do some of the cutting and taping ahead of time. Also, don't try to accomplish it all in one day. There are too many steps from the start of the project to the finished picture.

Store-bought Cameras   For convenience, you might want to buy cameras that use rolls of film. Remember, though, that kids are kids and prone to drop things from time to time. Don't expect them to take proper care of an expensive camera. We were able to borrow some old Brownie snapshot cameras and buy some more in thrift shops for 50¢ to $1.00 apiece. These cameras are sturdy, good for many hard bounces. If one does get broken, it's no great tragedy.

The biggest problem kids will have in operating these cameras is keeping their fingers away from the front of the lens. The shutter button is designed to be depressed by the index finger. To exert enough force to push the button with their index finger, kids will inevitably move their other fingers in front of the lens opening. To avoid this problem, show them how to hold their camera so that they can push the button with their thumb, grasping the camera body on the bottom with the rest of their fingers. In this position, it is almost impossible to get your fingers in front of the lens.

The other problem in operating the cameras is remembering to wind the film. Most of the cameras you find in a junk store will have to be wound after each shot. There will be a little red circle, usually on the back of the camera, that will show the number of the shot. After each picture is snapped, wind the film until the next number appears. We also bought a Hawkeye Instamatic Camera ($2.00 used), the kind that uses a film cartridge. This kind of camera has a mechanism which prevents you from taking the next picture without advancing the film. We let the kids who were not familiar with numbers use these cameras. Actually, most of the kids did a pretty good job of remembering to wind the film. When they forgot, there were some interesting double exposures anyway. You can avoid wasting film if you let the kids practice with unloaded cameras for awhile.

The first time that we used these cameras, we didn't give the kids any directions beyond operating instructions. We simply set them loose with their cameras in the park. Each kid had a different style as a photographer. One little boy spent a great deal of time arranging everyone's lunch boxes for a photo. He would set them up in a stack or line, step back a few paces and view them through the camera. Then he would come back and rearrange them. This process was repeated several times until everything was satisfactory; and he finally took his picture. Some of the kids followed birds around and tried to get close enough to get a big picture. Most of the kids made the independent discovery that things look bigger or smaller, depending on how close you stand.

When the pictures were developed and printed the kids made wall displays and books out of them. Some kids thought up ideas for books and then went out and took pictures for them. After the kids had used the cameras the first time, we would suggest ideas to them, like "take some pictures showing different ways that people feel." One child did this using another as her model. The pictures were a melodramatic series of laughs, sobs, and shivering fright. The photographer then pasted the pictures in a book with words describing the different emotions printed underneath. Once the kids were familiar with the camera, we let them take the cameras home and photograph family and friends. The possibilities are endless.

Photography is not an inexpensive pastime, but there are ways to cut the costs involved. Most of the simple cameras use 127, 126, or 120 film, which costs between 65¢ and 75¢ a 12-shot roll or cartridge. Developing costs anywhere from 75¢ to $1.00 per roll. Prints run from 10¢ to 20¢ apiece. These prices are for black and white. Color is about twice as expensive. Prices vary; so shop around for the best deal.

If you decide that you would like to do quite a bit of photography, you can save money by processing and contact printing the film yourself. For instance, it costs from $35 to $50 to have 50 rolls of film processed commercially. Once you have made an initial investment of about $6, you can process 50 rolls of film yourself for about $3. You can make 50 contact sheets, after an initial investment of about $1, for around $12. The set-up described in this book won't allow you to make enlargements, but the contact prints are large enough to enjoy. You can always have your favorites enlarged.

Once you have mastered the procedure, you can let the kids participate in and learn from the darkroom process. Although much of the work must be done by an adult, it's a magical process that really impresses kids. Of course, the involvement of the kids will depend on their ages and how cooperative they are as a group. The chemicals used in the photography are poisonous; so great care must be taken. I usually work in groups of two or three so that things don't get too hectic for me and I am able to supervise carefully. I have worked with kids as young as 2-1/2 in a darkroom. It's not really age that's important. The kids should be interested and mature enough so that you can work safely with them.

Film Making

Many of the super 8mm movie cameras are simple enough for a child to operate. We were given an older model by someone who had purchased a more deluxe camera and we were able to borrow another camera and projector. The cost of making short movies is not all that expensive, as low as $1.50 for a roll of black and white film and $3.00 for color. Processing for black and white costs about $2.00; for color, around $4.00. Shop around, since prices vary considerably. The film comes in 50 foot rolls in factory-loaded plastic cartridges. There are 72 frames per foot. One cartridge contains enough film for a screen running time of three to three and one-half minutes. Many cameras have frame counters so you can keep track of how much film you've used. Some cameras have automatic devices that determine the exposure which make them a lot easier for kids to use.

To avoid wasting film, let the kids practice holding the empty camera steady and squeezing the trigger. We began by taking films of the kids working and playing. Then, we showed them the films so that they understood exactly what kind of pictures this camera made. Soon they began to film each other putting on plays and generally fooling around. After the kids had some experience with the camera we tried some of the projects described below.

Stop-Motion

This film technique has been used since the earliest days of the cinema. It can be used to make objects and/or people appear and disappear in all sorts of comic and interesting ways. The effect is obtained by placing objects/people in a scene, shooting a few frames, stopping the camera, removing the people/objects, and then shooting a few more frames. When the processed film is projected on the screen the objects/people disappear as if by magic.

One group made a very clever film about a little girl and her fire engine using this technique. To begin the film, the little girl stood in front of a blank wall, and they shot a few frames. Then they stopped the camera and, making sure that the little girl did not move, they placed a red fire engine on the ground next to her. Then they turned the camera back on and filmed the little girl while she pretended surprise at seeing the fire engine and stooped over to pick it up. Just as she was about to touch the engine the director cried "freeze" and the camera was stopped again. The little girl held her position while the fire engine was removed. Then the camera was turned on again to film the little girl scratching her head and looking bewildered. The process was repeated several times. Each time the little girl was about to pick up the fire engine the camera was stopped. When the film was projected the audience saw a little girl standing against the blank wall, then, out of nowhere, a fire engine appeared on the screen. Much to everyone's amusement the fire engine disappeared each time the little girl reached for it. The film ended when the girl finally managed to pick up the fire engine. As she lifted it up, both she and the fire engine disappeared and the audience was left staring at a blank wall.

Two kids in our playgroup, Area and Jenny, made another very clever film using this technique. They called it, "Here Today, Gone Tomorrow." The film started out with Jenny, standing in profile, tapping her toe and whistling. Area tiptoed up behind her and tapped her shoulder. At this point, the camera was stopped and Area made her exit. The camera was started up again to film a confused Jenny turning around, discovering no one, and searching around for the mysterious tapper. The film went on like this. Every time Area tapped Jenny, she disappeared until, finally, Area did not disappear. Both the girls turned to face the camera head on. Jenny got a look of understanding on her face, snapped her fingers and disappeared, leaving Area looking bewildered and scratching her head. Finally she shrugged her shoulders as if to say, "That's the way it goes," and with that the film ended.

We also used this technique in a slightly different way. We took a cardboard box large enough to hold one kid. One child climbed in and we turned the camera on to film him climbing out of the box. We then stopped the camera, put another kid in the box and filmed him climbing out. We repeated the process with all the kids. When the film was shown, the audience saw kid after kid climbing out a cardboard box that was only big enough to hold one child.

When you are doing this kind of film it is important that the actors do not move while things are being placed in or removed from the scene; otherwise, the film will be very "jerky." Sometimes it helps to mark the spot where things are to appear, so you will know exactly where you want your objects or people each time. It is also helpful to have a tripod to hold the camera steady and to make sure that the camera angle is the same each time you stop and start.

Animated Films

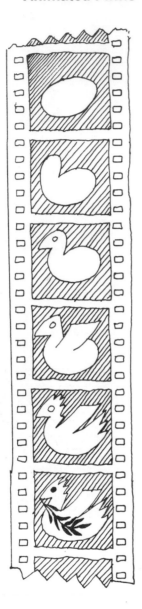

There are a number of different ways to use the stop-motion technique to make animated films. We took modeling clay and filmed it as the kids molded it into different shapes. Each time a new part was added to the figure, we removed our hands, shot two frames, and stopped the camera while another part of the figure was formed. If you try this, use a dark background and light clay. Too light a background will throw your exposure off and the film will be overexposed. Also, mark the position of the clay and the board or paper you are using as a background in case they are shifted accidentally during filming. Using a tripod will ensure the same camera position throughout the filming and will allow you to shoot down on the clay. Since we were careful to move our hands away before shooting, the ball of clay seemed to come alive in our film and magically mold itself into shape.

A similar kind of film can be made by filming a drawing in various stages of completion. We also made animated films by taking paper cut-outs and moving them around on a background scene that the kids had drawn. One of these cut-out films began with a few frames of the background—an underwater seascape. We used the stop-motion technique to make our paper fish swim around. Then a larger cut-out fish swam into our scene. Using a second copy of the large fish, only this time with a wide-open mouth, we made the big fish eat up the little ones.

It is a little difficult to judge just how much action you will need to shoot in order to create the illusion of animated movement on a screen. Sometimes it is quite simple. For instance, these three cut-outs, filmed in succession, will create a believable version of a walking figure.

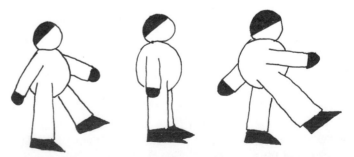

There are endless possibilities for making films this way. Animate some soup cans, your silverware drawer, combine human beings and inanimate objects . . . exercise your imagination and see what you come up with.

You may want to change the sequence of your film, or add or delete some frames. There are many ways to go about editing a film. Some photo shops will rent movie editing equipment. But, if you can't manage to get an editor, simply run your film through the projector, jotting down notes as to where you would like to make changes. Then, run the movie through again. When you come to the proper place, stop the projector, and snip off the shot(s) with a pair of scissors. Run another few feet of film through the projector. Then, you can splice the two ends together.

The easiest splice to make is called a wet splice. Scrape a narrow strip of emulsion off the dull side of the end of the film to be joined. Apply liquid film cement with a small brush to the scraped edge. Apply pressure for 30 seconds and then remove the excess cement.

There are a multitude of ways to make titles for your films. Expose at least five seconds of film for each title so the audience has enough time to read it. The kids can simply draw the titles and then photograph them. It is best to use light letters on a dark background. If you are using a light background you may have to adjust the exposure on your camera, even if it has an automatic device to determine exposure. The light background will reflect so much light that the letters will be underexposed and appear "bleached out." To determine proper exposure, you can use a "gray card" (sold at photo shops). Using your camera's light meter, get an exposure reading on the gray card and use that same exposure when photographing the titles.

By using the stop motion technique, it is possible to make animated titles. We made a title for one of our clay films by shaping letters out of clay and adding them one at a time, stopping the camera each time we added a letter. Shoot two or three frames for each letter so that the audience can read them. We finished the same film with clay letters that spelled "The End." The letters curled up on themselves and rolled back into a big lump of clay. Another film, made at the beach, ends as the tide comes in and washes away "The End" that we'd written in the sand.

It is also possible to insert titles into the body of film to explain the action or add dialogue as they did in the silent film era. Write your titles out and use a stop watch to determine how long it takes to read them. Be generous with the time, as some people read very slowly.

Editing

Titles

If possible, you should do these projects more than once. After seeing their first film, the kids will have a better understanding of what they are doing. The second film will generally be more fun, for the kids will be able to take over the project by themselves. Public libraries often have film collections that they will lend. Sometimes film rental companies have films that they allow the public to borrow for free and many of the rental fees are very low. If you are planning to make some stop-motion films with your group, try to get hold of a print of *A Chairy Tale* or *Clay,* both of which make excellent use of this technique. If you find that there are films available for free or at a low cost, why not organize a children's film festival in your neighborhood?

Animation Without a Camera

Animation depends on a phenomenon known as "persistence of vision." This term refers to the way in which an image "burns" itself on to our retinas so that the image remains with us for a fraction of a second after its source has disappeared. The toys described here, which were popular amusements in the Victorian Era, use this principle to create a convincing effect of animation without the use of a camera.

Despite its high-sounding name, this is a very simple device. It consists of a small disc with complementary images drawn on each side. Two short threads are attached so the disk can be spun, revealing the alternate sides in rapid succession. Due to "persistence of vision," the two images merge into one.

Thaumotrope

The flickerbook is another easily constructed toy. Each page of a small book contains an individual image which forms part of an animated sequence. By simply flicking the pages of the book, an illusion of movement is created.

Flickerbook

Zoetrope   This toy consists of a drum, open at the top and closed at the bottom, with a disc mounted by means of a bolt and spindle, so it rotates. Slots are cut at intervals around the circumference of the drum. A sequence of images like the ones in this book are inserted in the drum below the viewing slots. The viewer spins the drum and watches a succession of images through the slots. A convincing effect of animation is produced.

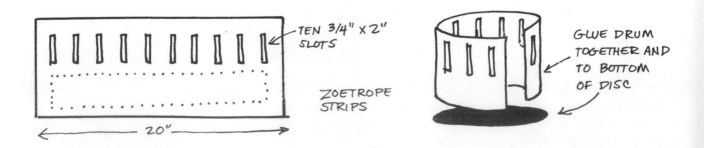

TEN 3/4" X 2" SLOTS

ZOETROPE STRIPS

← 20" →

GLUE DRUM TOGETHER AND TO BOTTOM OF DISC

The zoetrope slips here will work with a drum about 15" in circumference. The drum can be made out of stiff construction paper and a piece of cardboard can be used for the bottom disc. Before forming the drum cut ten slots about ¼-½" wide and 1-1¼" long and about 1" above the position that the strips will take in your finished zoetrope. A thread spool mounted on a piece of wood and a loose screw will serve as a spindle. For a smoother spin, try setting your zoetrope on a lazy susan or the turntable of a record player.

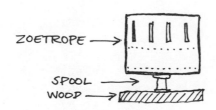

ZOETROPE →

SPOOL →
WOOD →

Theatre Games

Most of the games described here were suggested by actors and actresses. The games are used in theatre training to sharpen awareness of body, to exercise the imagination, and to understand how various postures of the body, expressions of the face, and movement of the hands and feet define emotion and communicate meaning. These games can help kids do the same thing. I especially like them for children because they stress cooperation instead of competition, and, unlike many games, there are no losers.

Mirror Game

Two people stand or sit facing each other. One person is the mirror or reflection of the other person's movements. If you concentrate it is possible to become an almost perfect mirror. Good players seem to anticipate the next move so that there is no lag in the action of the mirror player. The two kids pictured here are so good at this game (which they play with a serious concentration) that it becomes impossible to tell which one is the mirror. Sometimes they get so engrossed in the game that they, too, forget.

This game can be played with two or more players. The two teams are given an imaginary rope. Encourage the players to feel the rope. How thick is it? Is it rough or smooth? At the sound of an imaginary whistle, both teams tug. The idea here is not to win by pulling the other team over the line, but to exercise your body imagination. How are your hands and feet placed? What are your knees doing? Your back? Your mouth? Some players start with their bodies stiff and erect, only the hands showing any tugging motions. Encourage them to pretend until not just their hands, but their whole bodies are intent on tugging.

Like Tug-O-War, this game involves the imagination. The players spread out in a circle and toss an imaginary ball to each other. As the ball is tossed about someone calls out, "It's heavy; it weighs 100 pounds" or "It's light as a feather," "It's normal again." The players have to mimic catching and throwing an incredibly heavy or light or whatever ball. The game becomes really hilarious if the players can concentrate. It's one of those fun-for-all-ages games. Adults and children can play together at something they can both get into.

Playing Ball

Pantomime is the art of acting through wordless gestures and body movements. To break the ice, you might start with a group game. When we play this game, the kids gather around and someone, usually an adult, begins to narrate a story that everyone acts out. It might go something like this: "We're seeds in the ground and it's winter time. Now we're growing. It's spring; the ground is warming up; the seeds are sprouting. We're pushing through the ground. We made it; feel the sun. We're flowers growing taller in the sun, drinking the rain, sprouting leaves, blossoming. Our petals are unfolding. We're blooming. Perfume is oozing out of us. We're swaying in the

Pantomime Games

breeze all summer long. The hot suns of August are drying us out. It's fall; the weather is colder. Our petals are falling; our leaves are wilting; and slowly, slowly, the plants fold back into the ground." (To do it up right, put on some billowy classical music for a background.)

Of course, a flower is just one example; be an ant, a robot, a fish, a bird—anything, everything.

For solo performances there are simple charades games like "What am I doing?" To start, an adult or the kids might make suggestions for a pantomime— eating a lemon, climbing a ladder, drinking poison, waking up in the morning. The audience tries to guess what the actor is doing. Later on, kids can pair up or work in groups, collaborating on their panto- mimes, like the two girls pictured here who are pre- tending to be a motorcycle and rider. When the

audience has guessed, talk about what particular gestures helped you decide what was being acted out and how you used your body to tell what you were doing. Ask how others would have done the same thing.

For improvisations, a role and a situation are given and the players improvise action and dialog. It's easiest to start with situations that don't require dialog before adding the element of speech. For example: "You're a group of people waiting for a bus when it starts to rain. Only one of you has an umbrella."

Improvisations

Our group made films of each other playing this game. At first an adult may help assign roles and narrate a familiar story for the group to act out. Later on, kids will take matters into their own hands and do grand productions on their own. When this starts happening you will of course need a costume box with wigs, false moustaches, 1950's prom dresses, eyeglasses, old uniforms, garish strings of rhinestones, a clown's ruffle, various hats and a king's robe. You will also need a gigantic jar of cold cream, a box of tissues, and gobs of theatrical makeup.

Acting Out Fairy Tales

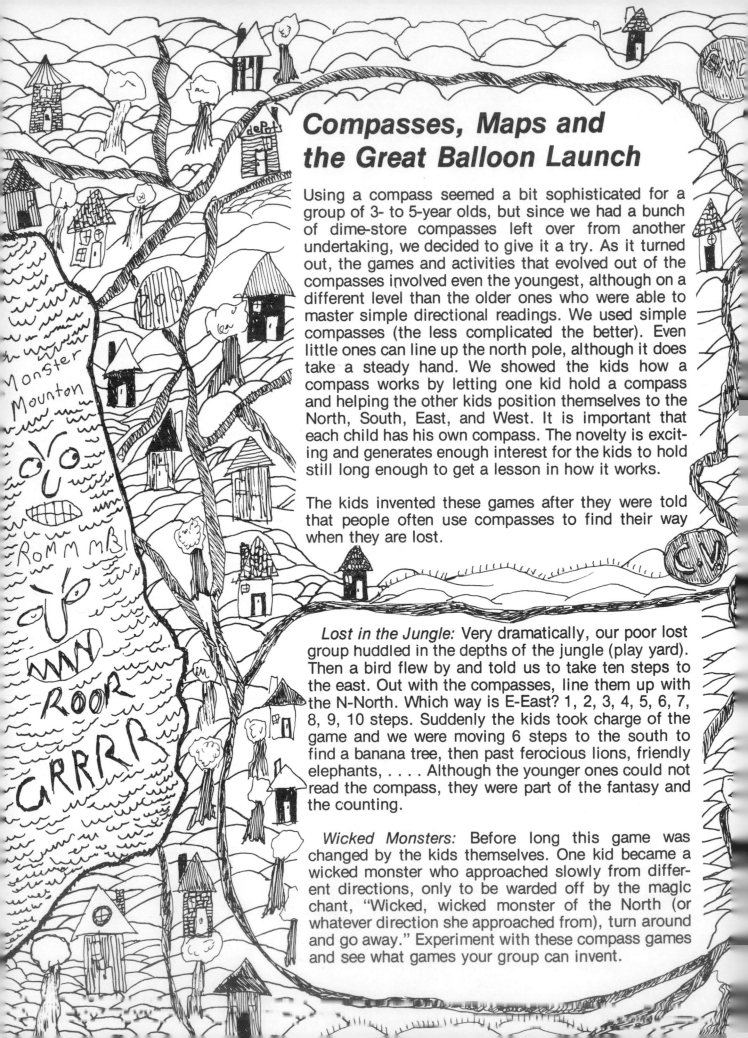

Compasses, Maps and the Great Balloon Launch

Using a compass seemed a bit sophisticated for a group of 3- to 5-year olds, but since we had a bunch of dime-store compasses left over from another undertaking, we decided to give it a try. As it turned out, the games and activities that evolved out of the compasses involved even the youngest, although on a different level than the older ones who were able to master simple directional readings. We used simple compasses (the less complicated the better). Even little ones can line up the north pole, although it does take a steady hand. We showed the kids how a compass works by letting one kid hold a compass and helping the other kids position themselves to the North, South, East, and West. It is important that each child has his own compass. The novelty is exciting and generates enough interest for the kids to hold still long enough to get a lesson in how it works.

The kids invented these games after they were told that people often use compasses to find their way when they are lost.

Lost in the Jungle: Very dramatically, our poor lost group huddled in the depths of the jungle (play yard). Then a bird flew by and told us to take ten steps to the east. Out with the compasses, line them up with the N-North. Which way is E-East? 1, 2, 3, 4, 5, 6, 7, 8, 9, 10 steps. Suddenly the kids took charge of the game and we were moving 6 steps to the south to find a banana tree, then past ferocious lions, friendly elephants, ... Although the younger ones could not read the compass, they were part of the fantasy and the counting.

Wicked Monsters: Before long this game was changed by the kids themselves. One kid became a wicked monster who approached slowly from different directions, only to be warded off by the magic chant, "Wicked, wicked monster of the North (or whatever direction she approached from), turn around and go away." Experiment with these compass games and see what games your group can invent.

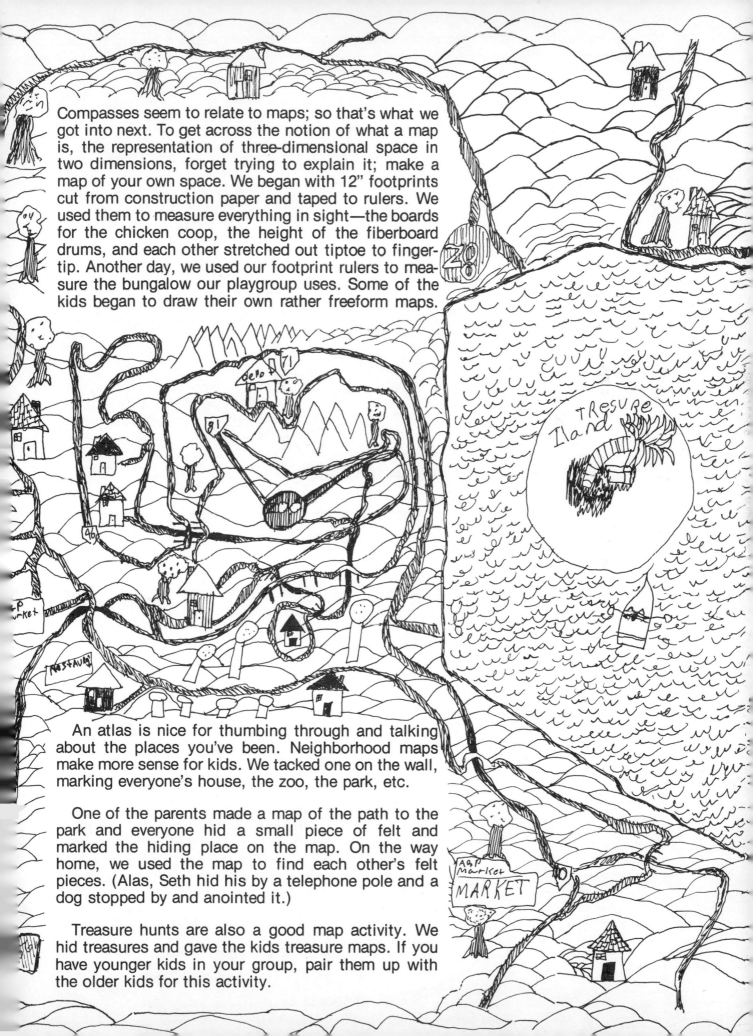

Compasses seem to relate to maps; so that's what we got into next. To get across the notion of what a map is, the representation of three-dimensional space in two dimensions, forget trying to explain it; make a map of your own space. We began with 12" footprints cut from construction paper and taped to rulers. We used them to measure everything in sight—the boards for the chicken coop, the height of the fiberboard drums, and each other stretched out tiptoe to fingertip. Another day, we used our footprint rulers to measure the bungalow our playgroup uses. Some of the kids began to draw their own rather freeform maps.

An atlas is nice for thumbing through and talking about the places you've been. Neighborhood maps make more sense for kids. We tacked one on the wall, marking everyone's house, the zoo, the park, etc.

One of the parents made a map of the path to the park and everyone hid a small piece of felt and marked the hiding place on the map. On the way home, we used the map to find each other's felt pieces. (Alas, Seth hid his by a telephone pole and a dog stopped by and anointed it.)

Treasure hunts are also a good map activity. We hid treasures and gave the kids treasure maps. If you have younger kids in your group, pair them up with the older kids for this activity.

The Great Balloon Launch

The climax of our map-making adventures was the Great Balloon Launch. We splurged on a tank of helium* and blew up 50 balloons to which we attached self-addressed, stamped postcards. On the postcards we wrote, "Dear finder, this card was attached to a helium balloon and released on October 18. If you find it, please fill it out and drop it in the mail. Thank you, Dirty Feet Playgroup. Where Found, When, Comments." Then, with great ceremony and picture taking, we released our balloons.

While we were waiting for our balloons to be found, we tacked a large map of the area on our wall so that we could mark the places where the balloons landed when the time came. As of this writing we have had two replies. One of our balloons went almost 100 miles in less than six hours!

*Helium gas is under a great deal of pressure and must be handled with care—make sure the tank is firmly supported (tied to a tree or post) so it cannot be knocked over by accident.

Scrap Cities

The city pictured below was made with wood glue and lumber scraps. I have done this project with several groups of kids, and each city was as delightful as the next. Sometimes the kids paint their cities with tempera and decorate them with magic markers. One group of kids made a scrap city after taking a tour of their own city, recreating the houses, highrises, factories, and so forth, that they had seen. Afterwards we unrolled some large sheets of brown wrapping paper and drew streets, railroad tracks, parks, lakes, etc. We then did a little city planning, laying out our ideal city with houses far away from the factories, "so the smoke doesn't come in your house." This kind of activity can open up discussions about what a city needs to live: Where are you going to put the garbage? How will you get water? Where will people work, play or go to school? How will they get there?

Growing Things

We explained to our children that plants are alive in much the same sense that people are. They move and live and grow just as we do. We got ahold of a time-lapse study of a growing plant. The photographer shot film of various plants over a period of several months. He then speeded the whole film up and, in a matter of minutes, viewers watched seedlings push through the ground, grow and blossom. If we had the eyes to see their incredible movement, perhaps it would bring it home to all of us that plants are truly "alive."

It may be that plants are capable of feeling emotions, just as humans are. Clive Backster, a lie detector expert, has connected plants to lie detectors. He has found evidence that plants respond to the death of other living creatures, to threats and to kindness. His experiments and other fascinating aspects of plant life are described in *The Secret Life of Plants* (Peter Thompkins and Christopher Bird, Avon, 1974.) Get a hold of this book and open yourself to new awareness. Meanwhile, spend some time around plants with your kids by trying some of the ideas described in the next few pages.

Vegetables

Raising vegetables is an exciting project, and even confirmed vegetable haters will eat their own produce. We had access to a small plot of land, and grew an amazing amount of produce. The kids helped with all sorts of garden tasks: fertilizing, hoeing, planting, weeding, and watering.

Select a spot as flat as possible that gets a full day's sun. To prepare the ground, weed your plot and turn it over with a shovel to a depth of at least 12 inches. Mix in fertilizer and rake smooth. Plant a border of marigolds around the edge of your garden. Their odor repels many insects that might damage your crops. Ask your local nursery for advice on fertilizing, planting, watering; and the varieties of seed best suited to your area. A good book for beginning gardners is *All About Vegetables,* edited by Walter Doty (Chevron Chemical Company, Ortho-Grow—Home and Garden Division, 200 Bush Street, San Francisco, CA, $3.98). The book includes lots of basic information and has different editions available for different sections of the country. Many nurseries will have free booklets, put out by seed, fertilizer and pesticide companies, which are very helpful if you disregard the poisonous chemical fertilizers and pesticides they recommend. No matter what your feelings about organic gardening, it's not wise to use pesticides in a garden project that involves children. If snails become a problem set out jar lids full of beer to stop them. Catch a bunch of ladybugs and set them loose on your aphids. But don't use dangerous chemicals around children.

You should not plant outdoors until all danger of frost is past. You can get a head start by raising the seedlings indoors. We started some in egg cartons filled with potting mix. Remember to label your seedlings since many young plants look alike to beginners. Put your plants in a warm sunny place and keep the soil moist. Transplant outdoors when the weather warms, according to instructions on the seed packet.

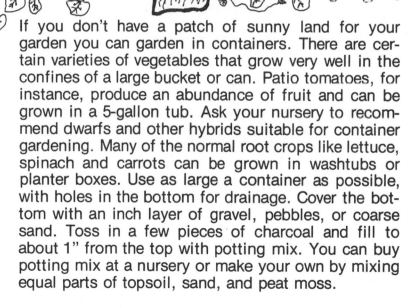

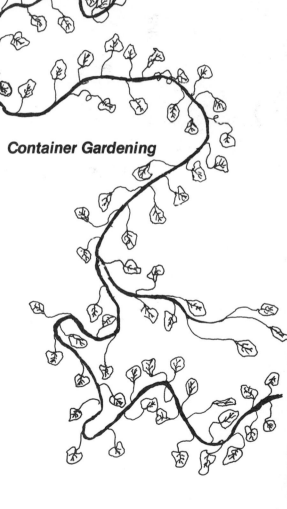

Container Gardening

If you don't have a patch of sunny land for your garden you can garden in containers. There are certain varieties of vegetables that grow very well in the confines of a large bucket or can. Patio tomatoes, for instance, produce an abundance of fruit and can be grown in a 5-gallon tub. Ask your nursery to recommend dwarfs and other hybrids suitable for container gardening. Many of the normal root crops like lettuce, spinach and carrots can be grown in washtubs or planter boxes. Use as large a container as possible, with holes in the bottom for drainage. Cover the bottom with an inch layer of gravel, pebbles, or coarse sand. Toss in a few pieces of charcoal and fill to about 1" from the top with potting mix. You can buy potting mix at a nursery or make your own by mixing equal parts of topsoil, sand, and peat moss.

You must keep your container garden in a warm sunny place, but if it is indoors or in front of a window, turn the plant once a day. Sunlight which passes through glass into an enclosed area can burn the plant and cause it to wither and die. Keep the soil moist, but not soggy. Normally, a good sized pot with plenty of peat moss should be watered two or three times a week. Because the plant is growing in a confined space, you will have to feed it regularly. I use a liquid plant fertilizer, diluted twice as much as the directions indicate. Use this once a week and you should have a healthy plant!

Garbage Gardens

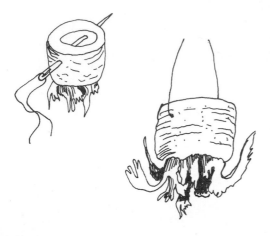

We grew these plants from things that normally wind up in the garbage can.

Carrot Top Baskets. Cut a 2-inch piece off the top of a thick carrot. Then scoop out the center, being careful not to poke through the sides or top of your carrot piece. Push a thick sewing needle threaded with strong thread through the sides of the carrot and hang the carrot so that the top is pointing down. Keep the hole that you have scooped out filled with water and watch the carrot grow new leaves. Notice that even though the carrot is hung upside down, the new leaves will grow up toward the sun.

Avocado Plants. First, wash the pit off thoroughly. Stick three toothpicks around the seed at equal distances at about 3/4 inch from the bottom (the broad end). Balance the toothpicks on the rim of a glass of water so that about 1/2 inch of the pit is in the water. Then put the glass in a warm spot out of strong sunlight. Check each day to make sure the water hasn't evaporated. As long as the water remains clear, the seed is fine. After a while (it might take some time) you will see some roots and then a shoot growing from the top of your seed. Allow the shoot to grow until it is about 7 or 8 inches tall, and then cut it in half. This directs the plant's energy into making a strong root system instead of leaves and stems. Two weeks after the cutting, it's time to pot your plant. Place the seed in a flower pot with a drainage hole that has been filled with a mixture of potting soil and sand. Make sure that your pot has a drainage hole. Only 1/2 of the seed should be covered. You can then place the plant in a sunny spot. Water daily and feed with liquid plant food every month.

Pineapple Plants. Cut off the top of a pineapple just below the place where the leaves come out. Let the top dry for a full day or the pineapple will rot before it roots. Then set the pineapple, cut side down, in a dish of moist sand. In about a month you should have a good root system. Transplant into a large pot filled with a mixture of soil, sand and peat moss. Keep it moist. If you're lucky you may get a pineapple.

Use your ingenuity to add to your garbage garden. In addition to these plants, try growing beet and turnip tops, sprouting orange and apple seeds, or growing a sweet potato plant.

Sunflowers are fun because they grow to such impressive heights. The giant varieties will grow 6 to 8 feet tall. We made sunflower houses by planting sunflowers in room arrangements. Get your gang together, pick a sunny spot and mark your floor plan on the earth. Weed a foot and a half border around the perimeter of your walls. Turn the soil over to a depth of 12 inches. Fertilize extra well. Plant seeds ¾ inches deep, 3 inches apart. When plants are 4 or 5 inches tall, thin to 8 or 10 inches apart. Normally sunflowers are thinned to about 20 inches apart but, to make dense walls they must be closer together. For extra dense walls and lots of privacy, plant a double row of sunflowers. If you choose to do this, the rows should be a foot apart. If your plants are too close together they will compete for root space and sunlight. Extra fertilizer should help. Sunflower houses are enchantingly private spaces for sitting quietly, or mazes for playing games. After the petals have withered and fallen off, cut the heads off the plants and hang them to dry under cover. When they have dried pick out the seeds and have a feast while you reminisce about your summer home. Or, let the flowers wither on the vine and you'll have a wildlife refuge where you can watch the birds that will surely come to feed on your sunflower seeds.

Sunflower Houses

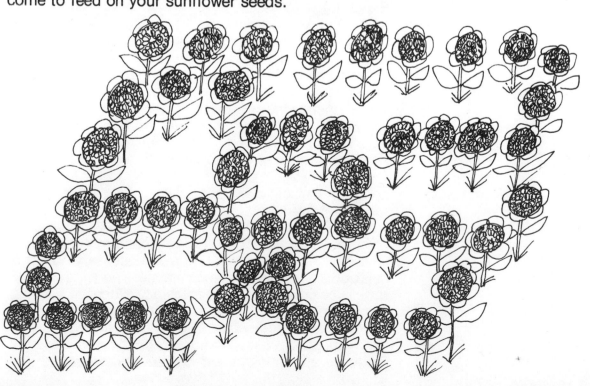

How Does Your Garden Grow?

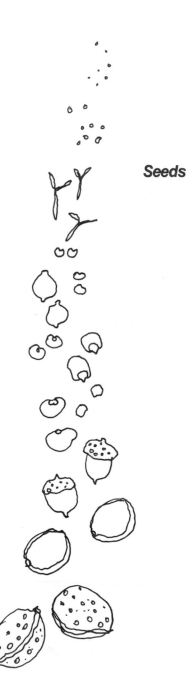

If you want to get scientific about it, here are some projects and activities that will help kids learn about how plants grow. Plants have a truly amazing anti-gravity system that allows them to pull water through their roots and up their stems to the petals, leaves and fruit. For a graphic demonstration of this, put a white carnation in a glass of water that has been tinted with food coloring. Take a look at the carnation every few hours; you will be able to see the path of the tinted water in the petals.

Seeds

Seeds are particularly amazing to me: their sizes, shapes and varieties are endless. Encoded in each of these fabulous packages is enough information to direct the growth of a plant. Inside the tiny acorn is the blueprint for a massive oak tree.

Split some seeds and look inside. Dried limas and mung beans are particularly good because of their size. After soaking the beans for several hours, slip off the seed coat and split them open. Can you see the baby plant? You can do some sprouting experiments by sticking a few beans against the side of glasses that have been stuffed with wet paper towels. Put one glass in the light and another in a dark corner. (Be sure to keep the towels moist.) Do both glasses of seeds sprout at the same time? Put another glass in the refrigerator. Do these beans sprout? Watch the roots and stems. How do they grow? Open a sprouted seed. How has it changed now that it is beginning to grow? Try sprouting alfalfa seeds and beans and eating them. We sprouted alfalfa seeds by putting a couple of tablespoons of seeds in a small mason jar. First, we rinsed the seeds and drained off the water through a piece of nylon stocking stretched over the mouth of the jar. Keep the jar in a warm dark place, rinsing them every day. When the seeds have sprouted, set them in the sunlight for a while and watch them turn green. Then, they're ready to eat— plain, or in a salad or sandwich.

Root Races

Building a root view box allows you to watch a special show. Days before anything shows above ground, you can see all kinds of action underground. The box is easy to build. Dimensions are not critical. Slanting of the horizontal side is necessary to force the roots to hug the glass or plastic. The window side should be covered with something, except at viewing times, since roots tend to grow away from a light source. Place the seeds 1/4 inch from the window so that you can get a good view of the proceedings. Radishes are an excellent choice since there is fast underground growth. There is enough day-to-day change to make radish root racing a real sport.

We placed our box in a warm sunny place and the race began . . . slowly and then more quickly until the green shoots finally poked through the soil. At a soil temperature of 75 to 80 degrees radishes will germinate in 3 days, beets in 5, carrots in 6. At cooler temperatures, radishes and lettuce should win by a big margin. If you build a couple of boxes, you can experiment with the effects of different fertilizers and soil, watering schedules, amount of sunlight, etc. Try talking or singing to plants in one box and ignoring plants in another. Do the pampered plants grow better?

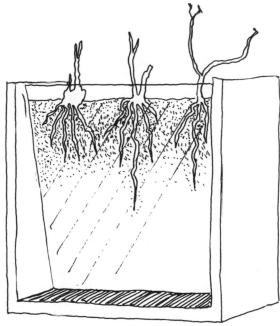

Moon Plantings

Farmers have been planting by the moon since ancient times. If you are keeping moon charts, you might want to try planting in accordance with the phases of the moon. Experiment with growing two crops under the same conditions that have been planted during different phases of the moon. My favorite gardening book, *Chico's Organic Gardening and Natural Living* (Frank Bucaro, Lippencott, 1972.) includes an index that tells which crops should be planted during which phase of the moon.

Happy planting, may you have a rich harvest.

Body Tracings

For this project the kids traced the outlines of each others' bodies on large sheets of paper. (This kind of paper is available in rolls at art supply stores for about 5¢ to 10¢ a yard. You can also use large sheets of brown butcher paper.) They then colored in their life-sized outlines. We helped them label body parts.

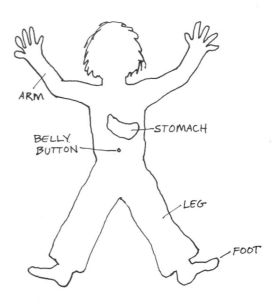

Body tracing may also be used to show what is inside the body. Sketch in heart, lungs, rib cage, intestines, etc. To enlarge on this activity, you can get hold of a stethescope and try listening for heartbeats. Can you feel each others' pulses? Can you sit very still and feel your own heart beat? After running up a hill how do you feel? This kind of activity can include trips to a doctor's office or a visit to the hospital or health museum. You could also try looking at *Me and My Bones* by Roy A. Gallant (Doubleday, N.Y., 1971). Also, try *What is a Girl?, What is a Boy?* by Stephanie Waxman (Peace Press, Culver City 1976) for body studies concerning sexual identity—the best book of its kind that I've come across.

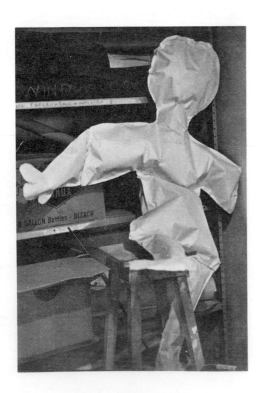

To take this project a step further, we cut two identical body tracings, stuffed crumpled newspaper between them and stapled edges together to make a life-sized doll. We also made body tracings that had moveable parts. First, we cut the tracings from large sheets of cardboard. Next we cut the head, arms, and legs from the torso. Then we cut the arms and legs at the elbow and knee joints. We punched holes in the pieces we had cut and joined them to the torso again with metal paper fasteners.

Insect Zoos

Since our kids, like most urban children, don't have an opportunity to watch the miracles of nature unfold in a natural setting, we tried to bring some of those miracles to them. Perhaps it sounds a bit corny to use the phrase "miracles of nature," but I can't think of any term that more aptly describes the birth of a butterfly.

Actually the kids came up with the idea of having a zoo when we were first planning our playgroup. It would have taken a wildlife refuge to accommodate their plans, but we did manage to find room for an insect zoo that allowed us to watch the life cycle of some common insects.

Ant Farms

I have made ant farms with several groups of kids and everyone found it fascinating. Each time there has been at least one child who was literally hypnotized by watching the ants tunnel and dig, and spent hours peering at them through a magnifying glass.

Building the farm: The first ant farm we made was a large glass jar filled 2/3 full with a mixture of sand and dirt. You will need to punch a hole in the lid of the jar so that the ants can breathe. To prevent the ants from crawling out through the air hole it is necessary to cover the inside of the lid with gauze or fine screen. In a day or two you will begin to see the ants digging tunnels. This kind of ant farm has one disadvantage: you can only see the tunnels at the edge of the jar, so you miss a lot of the action.

Our next ant farm was designed to let us see more. We made it from scrap lumber and two thin 12" x 18" panes of glass (cost $2). The dimensions are not critical, but the farm must be carefully constructed since the ants will exit through even the tiniest hole.

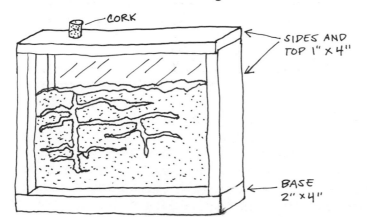

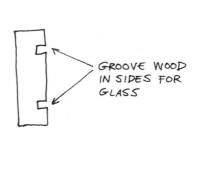

We made the grooves in the base and sides with a table saw. The grooves should be as close together as possible so that the ants' tunnels are not hidden in the interior of the farm. Ants do not need much oxygen; so the air holes should be small to prevent the ants from escaping.

If you are collecting the ants yourself, it is best to use the earth from their natural nesting place to fill the farm. Otherwise, a mixture of soil and sand will do. The mixture should be firm enough to support the tunnels, but not so hard as to make tunneling impossible.

Ready-made ant farms are also available. A popular one is made by Uncle Milton Industries, Inc. (10459 West Jefferson Boulevard, Culver City, California 90230). The kit, which comes complete with farm, fill, care and feeding instructions, and a certificate for a free supply of ants, costs about $6 to $10, depending on the size. It can be purchased in toy, hobby and pet departments or stores. If you can't find one, write to the manufacturer. Unfortunately, the ant supply does not include a queen, so eventually the colony will die off. Scientific supply houses also sell ant nests at prices from $7 to $13.

Finding Ants: Once your farm is ready you will need a supply of ants. The larger the species of ant, the better your chances are of keeping them in the farm and being able to see all their tunnels. The common grease ant that you may see in your kitchen is so small that it is almost impossible to keep them. One remedy is to set your ant farm in a pan of water. Barring disaster, ants will not attempt to leave an ant farm surrounded by water.

If you have trouble finding ants, contact entomologists at your local museum, college, or exterminating company. They will be able to suggest hunting grounds and may even direct you to a source that will sell you some ants of the largest species. If you collect ants yourself, make sure that they all come from the same colony; otherwise, they will kill each other. The kind of ants that build nests with mounds do best in captivity. An ant farm of the size described previously will support from 15 to 20 ants.

Finding a queen ant is a real challenge, but worth it. If you do find a queen, you will have a reproducing colony that will allow you to watch the entire life cycle. To catch a queen, locate an ant hill and set out

some fresh food to draw the ants. With a bit of luck, the queen may come out. She will be easy to recognize because she is usually about twice the size of the other ants and may have wing stubs left from her mating flight. If necessary, you can dig for the queen. With a shovel, carefully remove the top of the ant hill and set it aside so that you can replace it when you're finished. Then dig into the soft center of the next. Transfer a few shovels full of ants and earth into the bucket. Then with a small trowel, remove a bit of dirt and examine it carefully. This method will usually yield a queen. Refrigerating the ants for a couple of hours will make them sluggish and easier to transfer into your ant farm. Even if your colony does not have a queen the workers will still tunnel, but eventually the colony will die out.

Caring for the ants: It is best to keep your ant farm in a dark place or keep the glass covered with cardboard or cloth. Ants eat very little. Feeding them a few grains of cereal, seeds or a bit of honey once a week should be sufficient. If you are collecting the ants yourself, watch the ants in their natural state to see what kinds of food the ants bring back to the nest. Rather than cereal or seeds, some ants will eat other insects as their protein source. The ants will need water every other day, about 1/4 of a cup in an ant farm the size described above. It is best to keep one portion of the ant farm moist at all times. Don't be alarmed if some of the ants die during the first week. The other ants will cart the dead ones off to the ant burial ground.

Once you begin to watch the ants, a thousand questions about their habits, life cycle, and activities will probably occur to you. There is not space here for a discussion of all the fascinating aspects of ants. The library will provide all sorts of resource information on ants. A good book for both adults and children is *Questions and Answers About Ants,* by Millicent E. Selsam (Four Winds Press, New York, 1969).

Butterfly Gardens

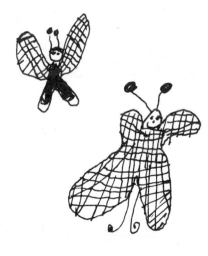

Butterflies go through a four-stage metamorphosis: 1) the egg, which is laid on the underside of the leaves of the specific plant that will nourish the hatched larva; 2) the larva, which we commonly call the caterpillar; 3) the pupa, in which the butterfly is protected by a cocoon or chrysalid; 4) the adult, which is the winged butterfly.

Collecting Specimens: Unless you know a great deal about butterflies, it is difficult to collect satisfactory specimens for your butterfly garden. Captured butterflies do not normally lay eggs. The eggs are very tiny and therefore, difficult to find and identify. Many species of insects look like caterpillars in their larval stage; so it is hard to be certain that you actually have a butterfly. If you are not sure of the specific species of butterfly, you may not be able to feed the caterpillar properly. Or, if you find a cocoon, you may have a long wait because some species spend several months in the cocoon before emerging as adults. Moreover, unless you can distinguish between moth and butterfly cocoons, you may wind up with a moth. Moths are generally active at night which makes them somewhat disappointing for classroom use.

It is not impossible to hunt up your own specimens, especially if you are armed with a bit of knowledge. If you begin with eggs or caterpillars, keep them in a jar with air holes. Feed them leaves from the plant you found them on, changing the leaves every few days as they will wilt. Provide a couple of twigs or branches for the caterpillars to attach themselves to when it comes time to form the cocoon.

For use in preschool programs, I prefer to buy Live Butterfly Culture Kits from Insect Lore Products (P.O. Box 191, Shafter, California 93263). They sell two species of butterflies, Buckeye and Painted Lady. Their most inexpensive kit ($5.00) contains 3 to 5 larvae in a sealed container with enough artificial nutriment to complete their development.* At normal room temperatures the caterpillars will feast for 5 to 10 days and then climb to the top of their container and hang upside down. Within a day or two they will have shed their furry coats, revealing irridescent

*Insect Lore Products sells a school kit with 25 larvae, nutriment, cage, and teacher / student guides ($16.50). They also sell a $7.00 Butterfly Garden that includes a coupon good for the $5.00 Live Butterfly Culture, a colorful cage, a feeding kit, and booklets of facts about butterflies and their care.

golden or silver tipped chrysalids. This pupal stage lasts for 7 to 10 days.

Building the Garden: At this point we made a cage out of a cardboard box with windows, covered with plastic wrap, on all sides. Then we laid the chrysalids carefully on the floor of the new cage. When they hatched, the butterflies crawled up the side of the box and rested there while they pumped their wings to full size. They do this by forcing blood into the veins of the wings. You may see some red liquid forced from the end of the tail. It is not blood, but the left over color from the wing formation.

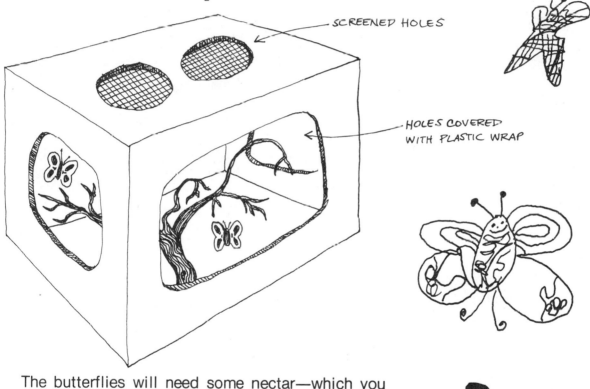

SCREENED HOLES

HOLES COVERED WITH PLASTIC WRAP

The butterflies will need some nectar—which you can make by diluting 2 to 3 teaspoons of sugar in a cup of water. To make a feeder, place a rolled up paper towel in a jar of sweetened water, like so:

It is possible to raise a second generation of butterflies by supplying the proper kind of leaves on which to lay their eggs. The Painted Lady should have bouquets of malva, although hollyhock leaves have also been used. The Buckeye will need plantain. Since we did not plan to raise another generation, we bid our butterflies farewell within a week of hatching so they wouldn't die in the cage.

Ladybug Hatcheries

The common ladybug has a life cycle that is just as complex as the butterfly's. The ladybug lays bright orange eggs no bigger than the head of a pin. Within 3 to 5 days after they are laid the eggs turn black and hatch. The larvae look almost like spiders. For several days they eat and grow until they begin to look like tiny orange and black dragons. Then they fasten themselves to a leaf or stem and bend double. For several days they do not eat or move. After this quiet period the pupal skin breaks and out comes, amazingly enough, a ladybug.

Finding Ladybugs: Ladybugs eat aphids—small light-colored garden pests that stick their sharp beaks in plants and suck out the juices. Ladybugs can be found in the spring and summer wherever the aphids are feeding (which as many gardeners will tell you is just about everywhere, particularly on nasturtiums, roses, sweet peas, lettuce, cucumbers, and weeds).

Building a Cage: For cages, we used clear plastic drinking glasses with air holes, set on a piece of cardboard that had been covered with a paper towel. If you want to hatch eggs you will need two of these cages. As soon as the ladybug lays her eggs, transfer the leaves to the second cage or the ladybug will eat them.

Care and Feeding: The ladybugs will need leaves from plants infested with aphids. The leaves should be changed every couple of days or when they begin to wilt. Simply remove the old leaves and paper towel and put in new ones.

We had a couple of magnifying glasses that were really useful. A good source for magnifiers and other math/science equipment is Selective Educational Equipment, 3 Bridge Street, Newton, Massachusetts 02195. They also make a capturing magnifier for viewing live insects that is excellent for young kids since it keeps the lens at optimal focal length from the viewed object.

If your group wants to expand the insect zoo, there are many other insects that can be reared in artificial nests. The best guide that I know of it *Rearing Insects In Schools* by R. E. Siverly (Wm. C. Brown, 135 South Locust Street, Dubuque, Iowa, 1962). It includes instructions on making cages, collecting specimens, care and feeding for many insects including crickets, grasshoppers, roaches, flies, mealworms.

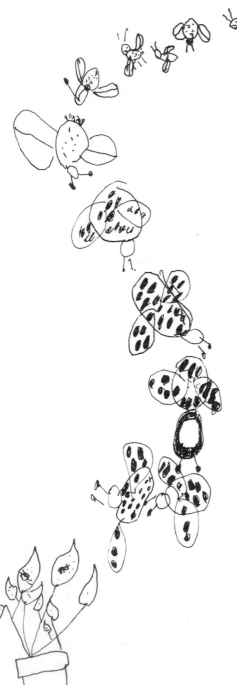

Adventure Playgrounds

When I was a kid, my playground was a wooded lot with a small stream running through it. I spent my childhood designing boats to float away in, building and unbuilding forts, and making mudpies with the red clay from the stream bank. These idyllic vacant lots are disappearing. In their places we have asphalt-covered, chain-link fenced city playgrounds at worst, or architect-designed, aesthetically landscaped play sculptures at best. But neither of these modern alternatives offers the opportunity for spontaneity, imagination and inventiveness that my childhood playground provided.

The snapshots here were taken by a friend from England who works in what they call an adventure playground. Instead of purchasing fancy swing and slide sets or building clever play sculptures, they use a vacant lot, hire a couple of ingenious adults to supervise and inspire and gather a bunch of kids. Using raw materials like cast-off wood, old tires, packing crates, and whatever else they can find, the kids construct their own playgrounds, raise gardens, tend animals and use their own creativity in designing playspaces.

If you have some outdoor space for kids, you might do better to forego swings, slides and other static pieces of equipment and let the kids create an ever-changing adventure playground instead. Try using some of the things below, all of which can be had for free, so that the kids can move them about and create their own playspaces.

wooden packing crates	barrels
vegetable lugs	wooden soda and liquor cases
rope or clothesline	beer cases
boards	pulleys
used tires	fiberboard drums
sawhorses	cable spools

Coat all cardboard surfaces with plastic sealer to protect from weather and remove protruding nails. If splinters are a problem, you might want to sand and/or paint rough surfaces.

H₂O

Water is a magical substance that covers three-quarters of our planet and accounts for 90 percent of our body weight. Kids have a real affinity for it and should have lots of opportunities to splash around and discover how it behaves. We scrounged lots of containers and measuring devices, splashed around a lot, and tried some of the ideas described below.

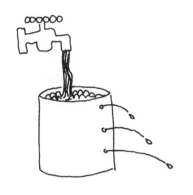

Punch a line of holes on the side of a tin can and fill it with water. Do you notice which stream of water goes furthest? How do the kids explain this phenomenon? We also had some fun with plastic tubing (available at hardware stores). Try placing one end of the tube in a bucket of water and the other in an empty bucket at a slightly lower level. Can you make the water move through the tube into the lower bucket? (Hint: to start the water moving, suck on one end of the tube.) What happens when the second bucket is raised higher? Lowered further?

Aqueducts

Heavy cardboard tubes split in half and propped up with forked twigs can be used to build an aqueduct system. Pour water in one end and watch it flow. Who used aqueduct systems and why?

Evaporation

Fill a container with water and mark the water level. Look at it each day, marking the levels as it disappears. Listen to the kids' theories of where the water is going. Is yours really any more sophisticated an understanding? Try boiling a pan of water; what happens? Where did the water go?

This experiment will convince some kids that you're a magician and others that an empty glass isn't empty after all—it's full of air. Stuff a tissue in the bottom of the glass. Turn the glass over and push it straight down into the water. Will the tissue get wet? Most kids will say yes and will be amazed to feel the dry tissue. Try it again, tilting the glass to the side so that the air can escape. After trying this magic trick a few times, some genius will notice the escaping bubble of air and figure out that the air was keeping the water out.

Displacement

AIR KEEPS
WATER OUT,
KLEENEX DRY

AIR ESCAPES
WHEN GLASS
IS TILTED.

We made our own bubble liquid by mixing liquid dishwashing soap with water. For super bubbles we used this recipe:

Soap Bubbles

1/2 cup Joy (use Joy, not a substitute)
1/4-1/3 cup glycerine (available at drug stores)
1 coffee can of water
1 pinch of sugar (to bind the mixture)

Use this mixture with giant bubble blowers fashioned out of coat hangers or pliable wires. Or, tie strings to plastic straws and dip into pans of super bubble mix. Swoop the straws and string through the air, making giant bubbles. Do you notice the colors in the bubbles? Wander around and find the air currents that will carry your bubbles higher. Try blowing through a straw into a cup of water and dish detergent. How do the bubbles arrange themselves when packed together? (Important—warn the kids not to suck in or they'll have a mouthful of soapy water.)

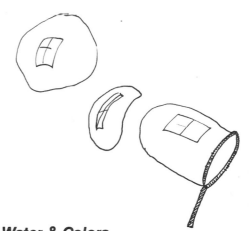

We gave the kids some bottles of food coloring, jars of water, medicine droppers (kindly donated by a pharmacy), and plastic type egg cartons. It is fascinating to watch the drop of color spread through the water in graceful swirls. What happens when you shake the colors and water? The kids also experimented by mixing different combinations of colors in the sections of the egg cartons. They began to discover what happens when you mix yellow and blue, how to make pale colors, and so on. Some of the kids painted pictures with the colors they made; others made "mixing colors" books to record their discoveries.

Water & Colors

Clay Boats   As they fooled around with water, the kids naturally began to experiment to find out what would sink and what would float. One day they were given lumps of plasticene clay and buckets of water. (Use plasticene, as other clays will fall apart in water.) The kids soon found out that the lumps of plasticene would not float, but one of the kids discovered that she could make a boat out of the clay that *would* float. Soon everyone was making boats. The kids loaded the boats with small objects to see how much of a load the boats would carry. The kids played around with the boats for quite a while, discovering how the amount and shape of the clay affected the boat's "floatability."

After a while, one of the adults pointed out how the level of water rises when the boat is put into the water. This led to a long discussion of "how the water in the bathtub gets higher when your brother gets in too" and lots of experimenting with the boats, loads, and water levels.

The kids were exploring sophisticated physics concepts of displacement/volume ratios, even if they didn't understand the mathematics or terminology that scientists use. This kind of "messing about in science"* provides concrete experiences that kids can draw on later in their education. Besides, it's fun.

This was a spontaneous set of discoveries, touched off by a lump of clay and a bucket of water. It's a situation that could be easily contrived. It's not a lesson to be learned, but a situation to be explored. It's also a fine example of how adults can extend a child's play simply by playing with the children and building on their spontaneous activities by offering the right suggestions and ideas at the right moment.

*It is possible to purchase classroom kits and teacher's guides for Clay Boats and other "messing about in science" experiments from Selective Educational Equipment, Inc., 3 Bridge Street, Newton, Mass. 02195.

Cubby Boxes

This project works well with kids who are old enough to use simple, child-sized hand tools, but even older kids may need adult help. If your group is too young, you may want to do the carpentry yourself or just use plain soda crates that the kids can decorate.

To make the box pictured above, we used a wooden soda pop crate. If the kids are old enough, they can cut a strip of wood and nail it to the middle section of the crate. Our group used precut pieces of wood for the doors, since the kids were not skilled enough to cut that accurately. Each door is attached to the crate with small hinges; the kids may be able to do the work themselves if you provide a child-sized drill and screw driver. Each of the doors on our cubby box closes with a different kind of latch. When the box is finished, the kids can decorate the interiors with all kinds of designs and surprises.

Measuring

Measuring things and comparing heights, areas, volumes, and weights is an activity that our kids enjoyed. Standard measures—feet, yards, cups, pints, pounds, and so forth—are rather sophisticated for most kids. To lay the foundations for later understandings, kids need lots of experiences measuring with various "rulers and yardsticks" of their own devising.

Length, Height, Width

Through their play and conversations with adults and each other, kids develop a vocabulary of length, width and height—long, short, tall, fat, thin, wide, longer, fatter, etc. When kids first begin to use these words, they may be merely naming things. For instance, "high chair" is the name of that particular piece of furniture. The tall cupboard may be the name by which adults refer to one cupboard, although to the child, all the cupboards are tall. As vocabulary and understanding increase, kids begin to realize that the meaning of these words is relative. Then they begin to get interested in comparing measurements.

We have a door frame that has a notched record of the kids' growth. Periodically, everybody lines up and has their height marked off. Everyone enjoys admiring how much they've grown. The experience of comparing your own growth and that of your friends can open up all kinds of discussion on height and comparisons.

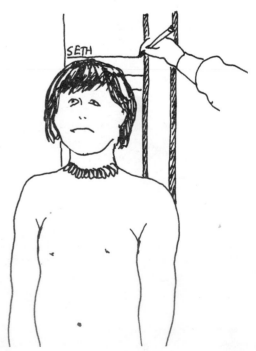

One day we took a ball of string and a long roll of paper and made charts. First each kid who was interested drew a line from his/her growth notches on the door frame to the floor. Then, the kids cut strings the same length as the lines. With a little help from their friends, they stretched the string out on a large sheet of paper cut from the roll. Using the string as a guide, they drew their growth lines on the paper, starting with the shortest string and working across the paper until they had traced their longest string/line. Then, as a final step they used their favorite color markers to connect the top of their lines. Although they didn't know it, they had made their first graphs, but they did know what that connecting line meant. It showed "how big I got."

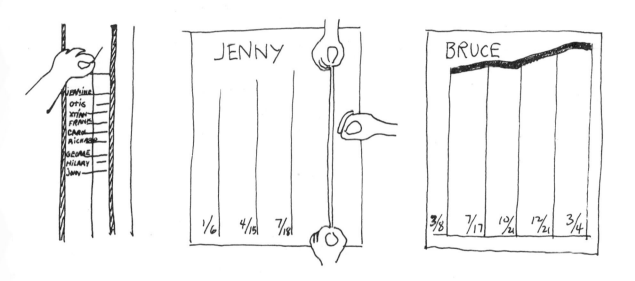

Kids can measure using all sorts of makeshift measuring scales. For instance, kids may discover that the play yard is 20 giant steps long; the block box is 10 handspans wide; Brigit is as tall as four orange crates; Sol is as long as 12 small table-top blocks. Strings can be used to measure circumferences. Our kids used strings to measure around each others' waists. Then they cut the strings to fit and tacked them on the wall.

After they've had some measuring experience, kids can begin to estimate before they measure. Some of the estimates will be outlandish guesses, but there is always a genius in the crowd who comes up with comments like: "It will take more of my handspans to cover the rug because my hands are smaller." or "It will take more blocks to measure me 'cause I'm taller."

Area   Measuring and comparing areas is usually left until high school geometry, but I've known some 4 to 5 year olds who can handle these concepts.

Geoboards are excellent for learning about shapes, space and areas. Kids can make geoboards themselves. Simply take a square of wood and lay out matrix of parallel lines equidistant from each other across the board and from top to bottom. At the places where the lines intersect, the kids hammer in a nail. All the nails should be hammered into the board so that they are approximately the same height. When finished the kids can define spaces and shapes by stretching rubber bands over the nails. The geoboards can also be made in a circular pattern. Standard size squares, rectangles, triangles, and pie wedges can be cut from colored paper and used as a means of measuring space on a geoboard. For instance, you might ask a child "How many squares do you need to fill in the shape you have made with your rubber bands?

Tracing the outlines of objects on graph paper and counting the number of squares covered is another way of comparing areas and discovering whose teddy bear is bigger.

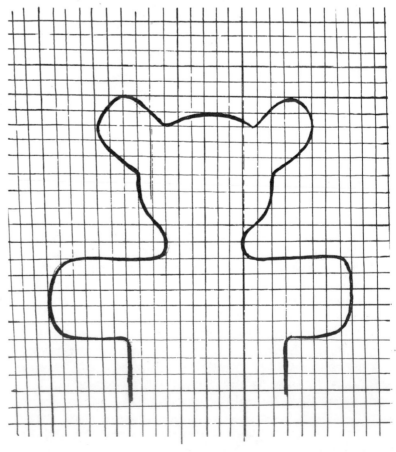

A supply of various sized containers and lots of sand and water will help introduce kids to the vocabulary and experience of volume and capacity. As kids gain experience with words like full, more and less, adults can begin to extend the experience by asking questions like "How many more?" "How much more?" Kids might enjoy making picture graphs like the one below which tells about one child's experiences pouring sand from one container to another.

Kids will enjoy standing on a bathroom scale and will demand to know how much they weigh. But, telling them that they weigh 44 pounds doesn't really have a lot of meaning for them. Balance scales are a better tool for introducing the concept of weight.

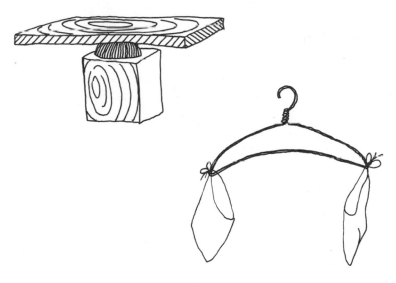

There are many different ways of improvising balance scales, some of which the kids can help build. We have also used a "first balance" scale made by the Selective Education Equipment, Inc. (3 Bridge Street, Newton, MA 02195). It's sturdy and attractive with easily adjustable sliding bolts for compensation of the balance beam. It also has a pointer to indicate balance. The cost is about $15, but it's a good piece of equipment.

Whatever kind of scale you use, provide kids with piles of assorted objects to weigh and compare. Let the kids discover what happens when one side is heavier and how to balance the scale. Cart it down to the sandbox and find out which is heavier—wet sand or dry sand? How many cupfuls of dry sand do you need to balance a cupful of wet sand?

Kids will enjoy recording their measuring experiences in pictures, charts, graphs, and stories.

Hi-Fashion T-Shirts

Everyone, from scribblers to more advanced artists can enjoy this project, especially since they get to wear the results. You will need white or light colored shirts (undershirts will do nicely) and a set of indelible magic markers. Pre-test your markers on a scrap of fabric to make sure they won't wash out. Slip the shirt over a piece of wood or heavy cardboard to prevent the markers from staining through the cloth to the other side of the shirt. Stretch the material until it is fairly taut and pin it to the board. This will eliminate some of the bunching of material when drawing. Then the kids can go to town decorating the shirts. Kids can also make these for presents, unless, of course, they get mercenary like my daughter. Her shirts were in such demand that she began to charge for them. Pictured above are some of her happy customers wearing their high-fashion 28¢ T-shirts.

Making Books

During the 50s, there was a best-selling book that asked the question: "Why Can't Johnny Read?" and answered it: "He can't read because the method of teaching reading is wrong." Then, of course, the author went on to explain his new and better method of teaching reading (which wasn't new at all).

The book caused a big flurry. National symposiums of teachers were convened to discuss the problem. Proponents of other methods wrote rival books. Attendance at PTA meetings soared. The issue received national press coverage. It even took on political overtones in the commie-fearing 50s (Ivan was apparently reading very well).

I wonder if anyone came up with the most obvious answer: Johnny couldn't read because he didn't want to. Dick and Jane were a bore. Who cared if Spot caught the ball? The emotionally sterile vocabularies of these readers—"Run, Spot, run. See the ball."—seemed deliberately dull, hardly designed to inspire enthusiasm and a love of language.

It would be a different story if kids wrote their own reading books. When kids tell their own stories, they talk about people, places and events that are meaningful and relevant to them. They use words that are charged, intense and personal. With their own stories in place of Dick and Jane, kids can get excited about words and reading. Even before they learn to read, they can learn how written language can be used to communicate their fantasies, fears, hopes, and ideas —if you'll help them to make their own books.

We keep a looseleaf notebook of stories dictated and illustrated by the kids in our group. They are funny, sad, touching, and sometimes revealing. Here are a few of my favorite short, short stories.

Leta's Story
Leta had a plant that died.

The End

SETH'S STORY

I had a Lot of fires not close to MY house. The last time Joey was there, he saw a fire starting, and it was a very quick one. Eight hundred and ~~ten~~ ten Fire engines came. They Put out the fire.

Jenny and Area's Fight Story

Jenny and Area were angry about Aunt Carol. 'Cause Jenny was calling " Goodbye Aunt Carol". 'Cept Carol is not her aunt. Area was angry so they started up enemies. We started up friends after.

Really elegant books can be made using bound sketch books available at art supply stores. These books have blank pages and hardbound covers in which you and/or the kids can create your own stories and drawings. Perhaps your kids have a fear of spiders or something. Why not write a story about spiders that can help inform them and ease their fears. You might leave space for them to do the illustrations. Catch a spider so you can get a look at it and count its legs so you get the right number in the picture.

Most people, big and little, are endowed with an absorbing self-interest. Why not make a special present for the kids about the fascinating topic of themselves. I made the book below for a friend of mine on his third birthday—a book about him, illustrated with pictures of him. Needless to say, he dug it. The book was made so that it folded up accordian style. It could be read by turning the pages like a book or strung out and hung on the wall.

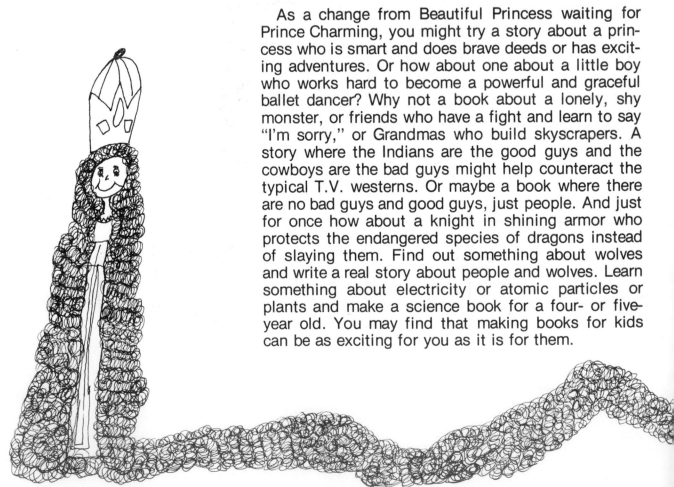

As a change from Beautiful Princess waiting for Prince Charming, you might try a story about a princess who is smart and does brave deeds or has exciting adventures. Or how about one about a little boy who works hard to become a powerful and graceful ballet dancer? Why not a book about a lonely, shy monster, or friends who have a fight and learn to say "I'm sorry," or Grandmas who build skyscrapers. A story where the Indians are the good guys and the cowboys are the bad guys might help counteract the typical T.V. westerns. Or maybe a book where there are no bad guys and good guys, just people. And just for once how about a knight in shining armor who protects the endangered species of dragons instead of slaying them. Find out something about wolves and write a real story about people and wolves. Learn something about electricity or atomic particles or plants and make a science book for a four- or five-year old. You may find that making books for kids can be as exciting for you as it is for them.

Make-it Box

A make-it box should be standard equipment in all preschools. It's like having your own private junkyard to sort through. It should contain material scraps, ribbons, lace, colored telephone wire, thread spools, pipe cleaners, toilet paper rolls, bits of glitter and dazzle, wood scraps, strings of old pearls, corks, paper clips, odd socks, rubber bands, leather strips, colored tissue, popsicle sticks, styrofoam cups, yogurt cartons, yarn, string, cotton balls, gummed stars, poker chips, felt scraps, metallic paper, rhinestones, acorn tops, egg cartons, strawberry baskets, sea shells, stamp pads, nylon stockings, clothespins, straws, tongue depressors, feathers, beads, and ten old Christmas cards. Of course, nearby you will need scissors, rubber cement, white glue, paste, hole punches, crayons, felt-tipped pens, magic markers, water colors, tempera, paint brushes, and fertile minds.

Arts and Crafts

I have not included many arts and crafts ideas in this book for two reasons. First of all, they usually bore me. As a child, I detested making lanyards out of plastic covered twine at summer camp, decorating potatoes with construction paper and tailfeathers for Thanksgiving and making popsicle stick jewelry boxes for Mother's Day. However, many kids enjoy this sort of thing; so don't rule it out unless it bores you, too. Secondly, there are already a multitude of arts and crafts books for young children: books on egg carton crafts, pipe cleaner crafts, seashell crafts, thousands of things to do and things to make. Check out the children's room of the library. They'll undoubtedly have a large supply of crafts ideas.

The books listed below are some of the best arts and crafts books I have come across. In fact, some of them are so good that even I, a veteran of summer camp arts and crafts workshops, got interested.

Making Things, by Ann Wiseman (Little, Brown and Company, Boston, Toronto).
This one is my favorite. There are over 150 pages of great ideas for improvising and creating delight out of readily available materials: weaving, printing, batiking, bread sculptures, stained-glass cookies, paper clip jewelry, plaster casts, musical instruments . . .

A Ball of Clay by John Hawkinson (Albert Whitman & Co., Chicago, 1974).
I particularly like this book because it tells you how to go about finding clay and how to prepare it for use. It always kills me to go to a school supply store and see a 5-pound bag of river mud with a fancy price tag.

Outdoor Art for Kids by Charleen Kinser (Follett, Chicago, 1975).
This book includes such goodies as windspinners, mud art, ice mold castles and incredible statues cast in sand. The photographs in the book are great too.

Beautiful Junk

Oh, I love trash,
Anything dirty or dingy or dusty,
Anything ragged or rotten or rusty,
Oh, I love trash!

The toys and creations pictured and described on these pages are made mostly from begged and borrowed junk. If you're working with a nursery school or co-op play group, you can outfit a lovely pre-school program for little or no money. Save what little money you may have to buy things you can't make. A record player, tape recorder, used video-tape or some other expensive piece of equipment will be more of a learning tool than a box of broken cheap toys.

Parents and friends making toys for kids will find that the feel of love and fun in the homemade toy—and the joy of making them—means a lot more than the plastic, mass-manufactured, store-bought toy. (I've seen an old cardboard carton provide more fun and draw more ingenuity out of a 4-year-old mind than the most expensive so-called 'educational toy.')

The ideas on these pages have been tried by my friends and I. They are only a beginning. Use your imagination. You can also get lots of ideas for toys from manufacturers' catalogs. Four good ones are:

Childcraft Education Corp.
964 Third Ave.
New York, N.Y. 10022
  * free *

Creative Playthings
Princeton, New Jersey
08540
  * 25¢ *

Childlife Play Specialties
1640 Washington St.
Holliston, Mass. 01746
  * free *

Pre-school Things Catalog
Pre-school Press, Inc.
159 West 53rd St.
New York, N.Y. 10019
  * 50¢ *

Another good source for ideas are school supply stores. Look for them under 'School Supplies' in the Yellow Pages. They will provide manufacturers' brochures for free.

Books such as the *Farallones Scrapbook: Making Places, Changing Spaces in Schools, at Home and Within Ourselves,* and the *Big Rock Candy Mountain* are also good sources for ideas about making things and about learning and living. For outdoor play equipment ideas, try the *Playground Book,* available from the Portola Institute, Menlo Park, California 94025, or write Playstructures, 432 Lakehouse Ave., San Jose, California 95110.

Get your kids to join in designing and making their toys from the free and low cost materials which surround us. The process is enjoyed by all, and teaches us many important lessons. The results will please more — and last longer than — the expensive items we have come to rely upon.

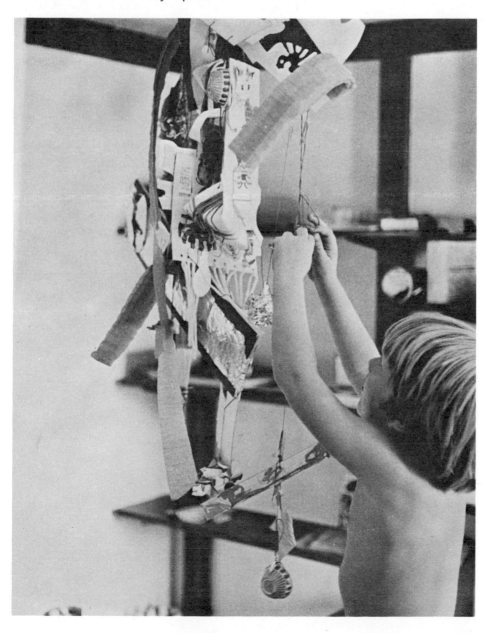

Playgrounds

Most of these toys are for out-of-doors, although some can be used inside if you have a big enough space. The cardboard ones, of course, must be protected from the weather.

Tunnels

A section of sewer pipe makes a great tunnel. Keep your eyes open for yours. You can sometimes get them from a construction crew or from the city or state department that is responsible for the sewer systems. Remember that any tunnels you make must be short enough and big enough to allow adults to reach the children easily.

Large appliance crates put end to end make a fine tunnel when you cut passage ways in the ends of the boxes.

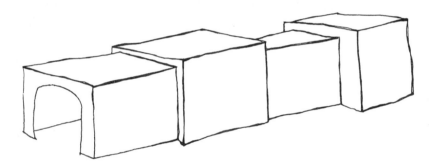

Box Cities

If you can find a way to cart them away, stove and refrigerator crates can form a beautiful box city. Simply cut windows and doors, give the kids some brushes and buckets and let them paint the town.

Utility and phone companies will give away empty cable spools. But, don't call the president of the company to ask for one. Go down to the 'yard' where they are kept and ask the people working there. The cable spools come in several sizes from one to seven feet in diameter.

Cable Spools

Sanded down, cable spools make great tables. If you cut the cross bracing in half, the big ones become the perfect height for pre-schoolers.

You can make a climbing toy by cutting the top and bottom circles of one of the large cable spools so that it rests flat on the ground. Nail a climbing plank to the spool and paint lavishly.

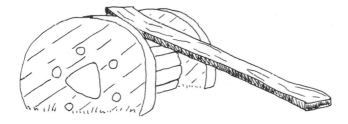 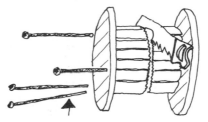

Fiberboard drums are fun to roll around in and over. They can be transformed into spaceships with or or without a nose cone. Empty ice cream containers (from restaurants or Ice cream parlors) make matching space helmets with a slit visor. Paint both silver on a sunny day.

Fiberboard Drums

Tire Toys Used tires are a safe and inexpensive building material. In trade for a six-pack of beer I received a life-time unlimited supply from a local tire recapping place. You might also try your neighborhood gas stations.

We painted a load of tires and laid them on a hillside into which we had sunk a slide. Drill holes into the tires so that rainwater will escape.
We made this climbing toy by simply stacking tires on a pole that had been sunk 6 feet into the ground.

The possibilities for creating tire structures are unlimited. Support poles should be sunk at least 6 feet into the ground. Tires can be joined with 3/8" by 2" cap screws. To prevent the screws from pulling through the tires use a 3/8" fender washer and a 3/4" steel washer on each side of the joined tires. Use a 7/16" drill bit to drill holes in the tires. Joining will be easier if you use tires of the same rim size. Push the steel washer, fender washer and cap screw through both tires. Place another set of washers over the end of the screw and fasten the joint with a 3/8" nut. For suspended tires where the joint is under pressure, use a lock washer and a second nut to prevent the bolt from loosening.

These suspended tire structures are held together with 1/4" chain. Wrap the chain around the tire and bolt it together. When attaching the tires to the support structure, make sure the chain is not too tight or it will tend to snap. To prevent the chain from wearing away at the support structure, nail a sleeve of tire around the beam or pole where the chain is attached. For vertical supports, lag bolts or 3" fence staples with the ends protruding will do nicely.

This jungle gym was inspired by the *Farallones* Scrapbook — an excellent book with lots of junk toy ideas. It bolts together easily with 1¼-inch length 5/16 bolts.

If you can find some of those huge tires from a tractor, trucker's rig, or any heavy duty vehicles, they make great climbing toys too.

An old standard is the tire swing. If you have a convenient tree limb, one section of solid rope and one tire, you are set. Tie the rope so that you don't strangle the limb.

If you can find one of those super wide tires with worn tread, try making this fancy version of a tire on a rope. For extra comfort, you can add a foam cushion with a waterproof cover.

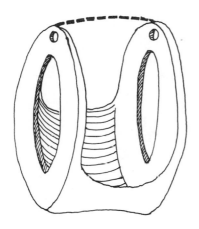

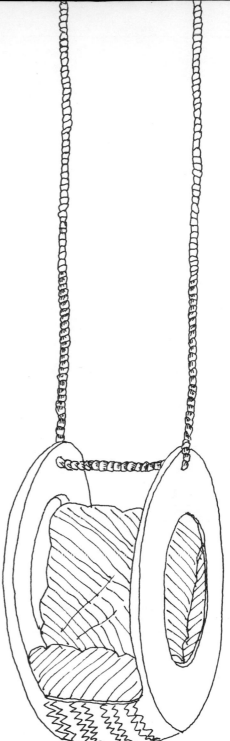

All that you need for this tire coaster is one used tire, four pieces of 4 x 4's long enough to wedge tightly inside the casing, four casters, wood screws and washers.

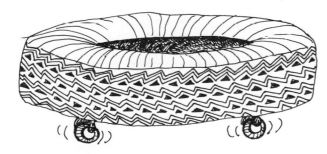

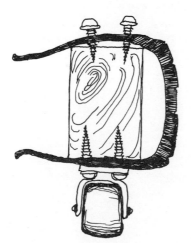
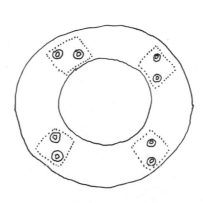

Cardboard Carpentry

Cardboard can be as sturdy as wood if it is thick enough. Single wall, the kind we find in ordinary boxes, is not too strong and bends easily. Tri-wall (3-layers) is comparable to wood in strength. It can be made by gluing sheets of single wall together with white glue or rubber cement. Slap the pieces together and weigh them down until they dry. Large sheets of free single wall are available from furniture stores. A 4' x 6' sheet of tri-wall costs about $2.

Working with tri-wall is a joy: to make a neat bend, notch a groove in the board, and bend; joining two pieces takes only a notch in each piece.

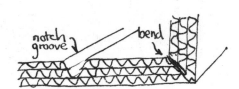

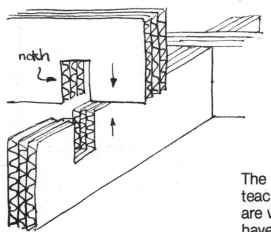

The Workshop for Learning Things is a group of teachers, photographers, writers and designers who are working to reshape classroom environments. They have printed a couple of books with drawings, plans, and photos of magnificent cardboard creations. You can obtain their catalog by writing to them at 5 Bridge Street, Watertown, Massachusetts 02172.

In addition to the slide and ladder house pictured on these pages, these folks produce and sell cardboard carpentry tools and threaded wood dowels and nuts which can be used to assemble your cardboard creations.

This slide is made of cardboard and stands about three feet high. It is assembled using the threaded birch dowels and wood nuts, and is light enough for kids to lug around.

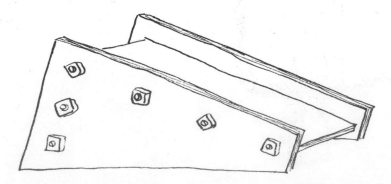

This Ladder House can be used flat on the floor as a crawl-through or upright as a climbing tower. It's made with folded tri-wall and long, stout birch threaded dowels and wood nuts.

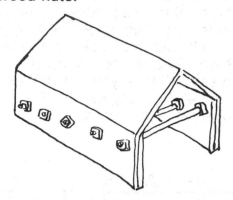

They call this a Tetter-Go-Round. It's a see-saw that goes around as well as up and down. It has a heavy cast iron base and hard rubber landing wheels. The arms are of 2" fir.

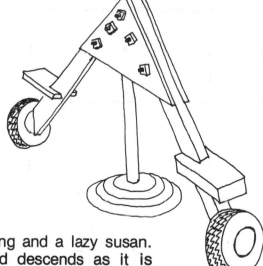

This is a combination of a swing and a lazy susan. The Twista-Go-Round rises and descends as it is wound round and round.

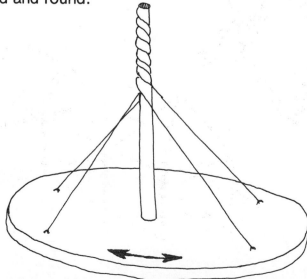

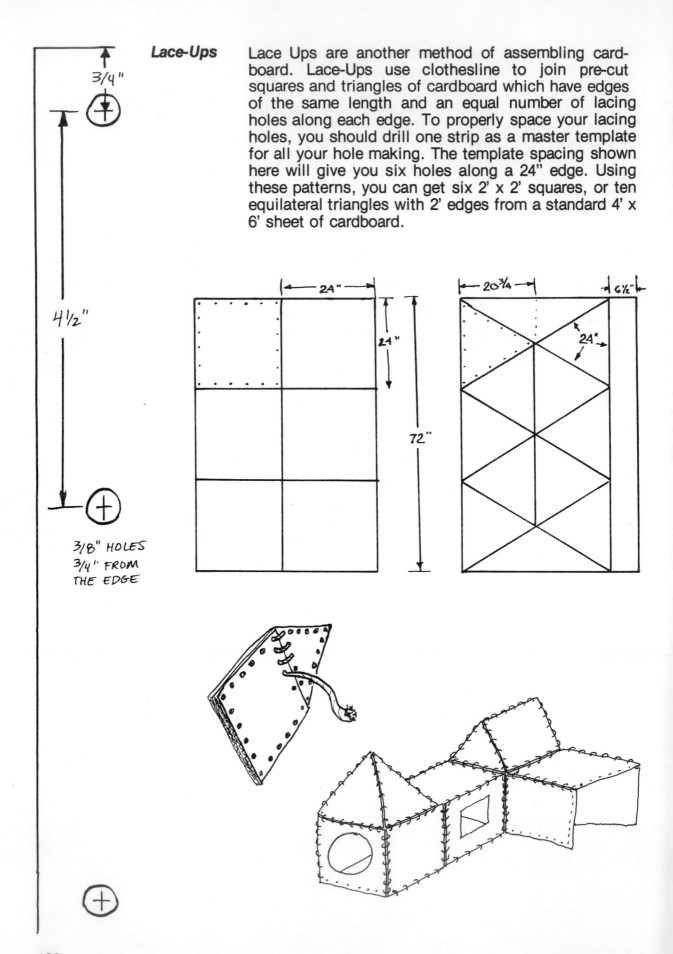

Lace-Ups

Lace Ups are another method of assembling cardboard. Lace-Ups use clothesline to join pre-cut squares and triangles of cardboard which have edges of the same length and an equal number of lacing holes along each edge. To properly space your lacing holes, you should drill one strip as a master template for all your hole making. The template spacing shown here will give you six holes along a 24" edge. Using these patterns, you can get six 2' x 2' squares, or ten equilateral triangles with 2' edges from a standard 4' x 6' sheet of cardboard.

3/4"

4½"

3/8" HOLES
3/4" FROM
THE EDGE

24"

24"

72"

20¾"

6½"

24"

Lace-Ups can be also be used to learn about many geometric solids. Most kids have had experience with spheres and cubes — but how about creating some of the solids pictured here? To construct these geodesic solids, lay the pieces flat on the floor in the patterns illustrated and lace the touching edges. When you lift the partially laced form the unlaced edges will fall in place, and it will be easy to lace them together.

TETRAHEDRON
4 TRIANGES

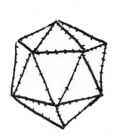

ISCOSAHEDRON
20 TRIANGLES

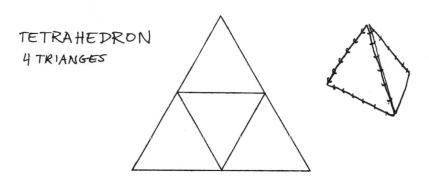

CUBOCTAHEDRON
8 TRIANGLES + 6 SQUARES

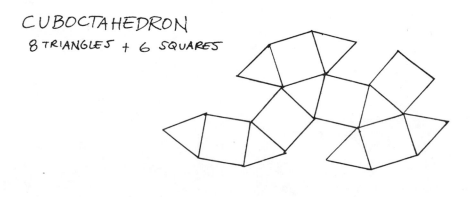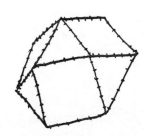

Geodesic Jungle Gym

A very inexpensive geodesic jungle gym can be made if you can track down any surplus or scrap aluminum tubing. We were able to purchase one-inch, light-weight, medium-hard alloy for 5¢ a foot.

The jaw-breaking terminology for this design is a "two frequency alternate icosahedral geodesic hemi-sphere." To construct a jungle gym with a ten-foot diameter, and a high point of five feet off the ground, you will need: 30 2'10¾" struts, and 35 3'3" struts.

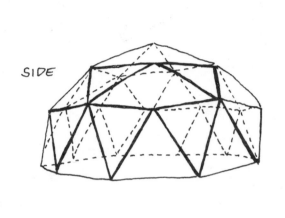

SIDE

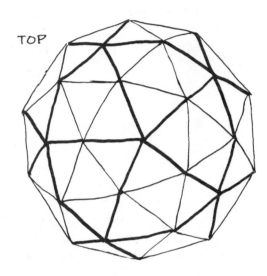

TOP

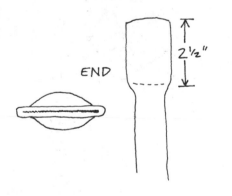

END

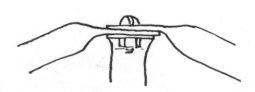

In order to drill and connect these struts, you will have to flatten the ends about 2½" from the tip of each pipe. Do this with a vise, or even by pressing the ends between two boards, but get them as flat as possible.

Once flattened, you must drill holes for the bolts used to hold the dome together. These holes must be big enough for your bolts, and will be approximately one inch from the ends of each strut, but should be as close as you can make it to: 2'8¾" from hole to hole on the short struts, and 3'1/16" from hole to hole on the long struts. (Buy round head bolts that will be just long enough to go through six of your flattened struts.)

2½"

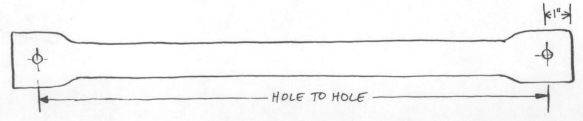

1"

HOLE TO HOLE

The assembly of your geodesic jungle gym is best done by using a pattern; otherwise it can get a bit confusing. A simple pattern is:

1. Lay out the thirty short struts and temporarily bolt them together.
2. Add long struts to close the six pentagons, and temporarily bolt them together. You will note that you will have to lift the center and effect a slight bending of each strut in order to close the pent.
3. If you now pick up this structure from the ground by the center pent, you will see the five surrounding pents draw close to one another and touch their neighbors. Fasten these five points together.
4. Insert the remaining five struts along the bottom course.
5. Tighten all the bolts down, and you are finished.

If you are intrigued by this structure — and you are certainly bound to be if you do construct it — you may wish to look at Domebook 2, a popular handbook on geodesics. It covers a wide range of topics, from geodesic theory and model building through some small home architectural efforts.

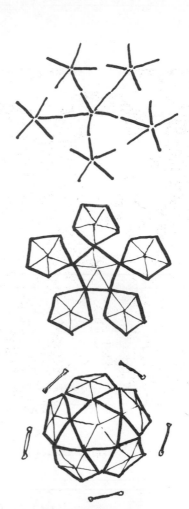

Musical Instruments

The simple percussion instruments illustrated on these pages can be the basis for a swinging rhythm section. Playing in a rhythm band is a way of learning about listening: to music, to rhythms, and to each other.

If you play an instrument, or have a friend who does, make up simple songs for the kids to boom and click with. Libraries sometimes have rhythm band records you can borrow. Don't be discouraged if it is a lot of noise at first; keep on jamming and it will fall together.

Start out by letting the kids explore the sounds the instruments can make. Listen to a recording of Peter and the Wolf, in which each major character is associated with particular instruments and musical patterns. Then play a game where the kids characterize animals and people with these:

Wrist or Ankle Bells

Attach 3 or 4 small jingle bells to a 9" strip of leather or elastic. Sew the ends together, and attach to dancing bodies.

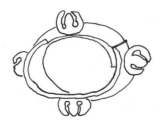

Rhythm Sticks

Rhythm sticks can be made from wooden dowels, a discarded broom handle, or even a branch. Cut sticks into lengths between 8 and 12 inches, and sand any splintery surfaces smooth. Different woods, lengths, and thicknesses will give you different sounds, so experiment. You might try using these to play along with recordings of African tribal music.

An interesting variation can be made by notching one of your sticks at regular intervals (like every ¼" or ½") with a saw or a file. Scraping a smooth stick up and down the notched one makes a cricket-like sound.

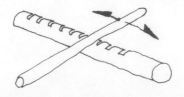

Rhythm blocks require only two scraps of wood about 4" x 5", and two smaller pieces for handles. Glue the handles to the blocks with a little white glue and pressure. A strip of leather or elastic could be substituted for the wooden handles.

Rhythm Blocks

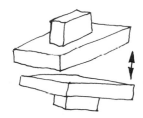

Sand blocks are made by adding medium grade sandpaper to the faces of rhythm blocks. Cut the paper so that it folds around two edges of the blocks. Glue the paper's smooth side to the block, and fold the ends up. Drive two staples in each end.

Sand Blocks

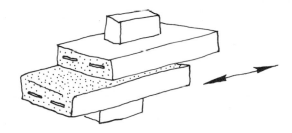

Mark a clean, dry gourd in order to match the halves together later on. Cut the gourd in half. Scrape out the seeds and let the gourd dry. Don't try to scrape out all the meat, or the gourd will 'pucker up' as it dries. Sand when dry. Then, add a few beans, rice, etc., and glue one half of the gourd to a piece of white tagboard — the type of cardboard that comes in shirts from a laundry. This board acts like a drum head. When dry, trim the excess tagboard away. Then glue the other half of the gourd, which has also been filled with its own beans, to the piece of tagboard. Use the mark to line up the halves. Dry. Boogie.

Gourd Maracas

Tom-Tom   A coffee can tom-tom can be made from a coffee can, an inner tube, and a piece of clothesline. Cut two circles larger than the top of the coffee can from the inner tube. Punch holes around the circle. Be careful not to punch too close to the edge, or it will tear. Try to have the same number of holes on both heads. And lace up the drum with the clothesline, top, bottom, top, bottom, . . . 'til the ends meet, and tie them off.

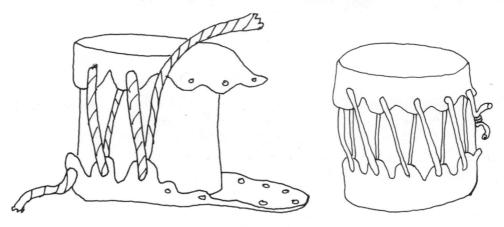

Jingle Stick   Clean two soda bottle caps, and punch a hole through the center of each with a fat nail. Attach the caps to a 5" length of 1" wood dowel (such as an old broom stick — or wood scrap) using a round head, 1¼" wood screw. Be sure that the caps move freely on the screw, and have enough play to generate some noise.

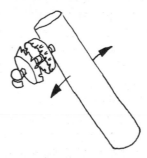

Jingle Ring   Clean and punch 10 soda caps as above. Cut a piece of wire from a coat hanger and string the caps onto the wire. Bring the ends together and twist. Bend the twisted wire down to meet the loop, and cover the twist with tape (or shellacked twine) to protect little hands.

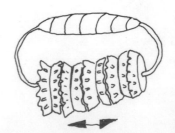

Fill empty metal spice cans or pill boxes with beans, rice, etc., and snap shut. You might wish to paint these with a non-toxic paint to prevent the kids from playing with your non-empty spice or pill boxes. Seal well with cloth tape.

Spice-Can Rattle

Toss a handful of soda caps, rice, or other noisy things into a discarded aluminum pie pan. Cover with another pie pan, and staple (or tape) the edges together.

Tambourine

Metal objects: spoons, pans, buckets, hub caps, pipes, garbage can lids, etc. . . . can be used to make a lovely orchestra. Tie your collection to a clothesline strung between poles, give your conductor a wooden spoon, and let the music begin.

Symphony Orchestra

You can add to your rhythm band with some of the old standards — strumming a washboard, playing a comb and wax paper, blowing across the top of soda bottles, or tapping glasses with varying amounts of water.

If your group gets excited by making and playing these simple instruments, you may want to try some more sophisticated junk instruments. A beautiful book called the Musical Instrument Recipe Book has directions for making such goodies as Garden Hose Recorders, Beach-Bottle Banjos and Tongue Depressor Finger Pianos . . . it can be ordered from the McGraw-Hill Book Company.

Puzzles

There are lots of puzzles on the market — some really lovely ones, but it is hard to justify their expense, since once they are mastered, interest dies fast. Besides, if you lose one piece, the puzzle is shot. Inexpensive cardboard puzzles are available, but unfortunately many of these are poorly made and can cause a lot of frustration because their parts do not fit together easily. They are cut poorly or have a tendency to buckle, and often have to be pounded into place.

Some children are fascinated by puzzles, while others couldn't be bothered. You should experiment to find out if yours enjoy this kind of problem solving before you launch into any full scale manufacturing.

Form Puzzle   A simple puzzle can be made by cutting out basic forms from a piece of cardboard (such as squares, circles, triangles, etc.). The puzzle pieces can be painted by the children. You may have to trim the edges slightly so that little fingers can slide the pieces in and out easily. The puzzle must be worked on a flat surface, as it has no backing.

This slightly fancier puzzle is more interesting when a favorite drawing or picture is used.

Picture Puzzle

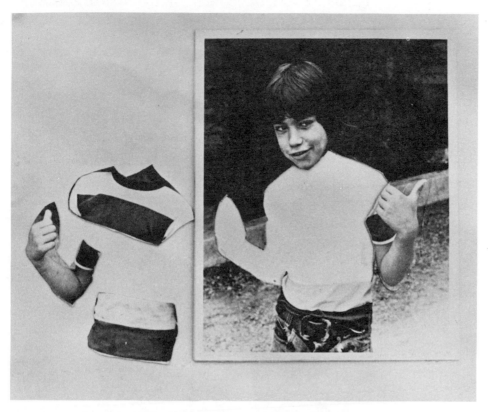

A mat knife or razor knife can be used to cut out the puzzle's pieces. As before, you may have to trim the edges of the pieces to assure an easy fit. As the child grows, puzzles can be made more complex by increasing the number of pieces. Puzzles will last longer if you add a back to their frame. This helps to retain the pieces when not in use. (Do be sure to glue only the *frame* to the back!)

Oriental Puzzle   This geometric puzzle is reputedly an ancient Chinese game which consists of five triangles, one square and one parallelogram, which can be assembled together as a large square. It can be made by simply tracing this pattern onto wood or cardboard, and cutting out the pieces. The pieces can also be used to make other designs.

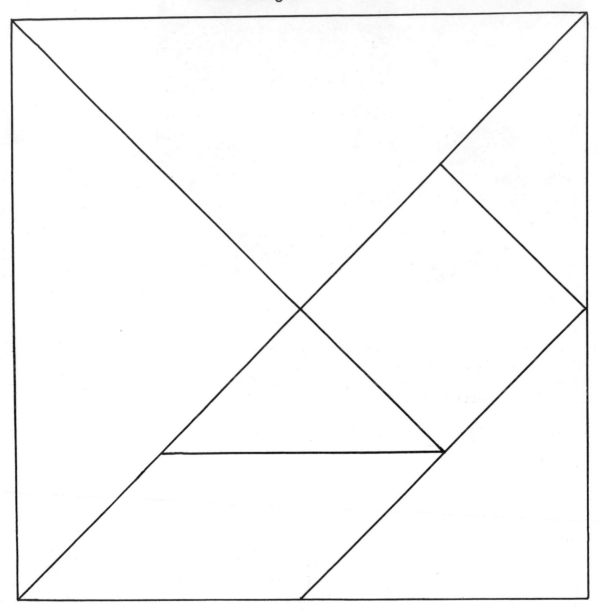

This puzzle can be made from either 25 wooden cubes laid out in a square five rows of five, or 16 cubes in a square of four rows of four. The fewer-block version makes a simpler puzzle for younger kids. When completed, all six sides of each cube are covered with a portion of six different pictures. To solve the puzzle, the blocks must be placed in a square which forms one of the six possible solutions. If you don't happen to have 25 cubes laying around the house, you can buy a short section of 2 x 2, and cut off as many cubes as you need. Assemble the blocks in a square, and hold them together with a rubber band. Apply white glue to the surface of the blocks, and firmly and smoothly press the picture in place. Lightly mark the picture over the block joints, and cut the picture along these lines with a razor. Assemble the blocks into another square with blank faces up — glue and cut as before — repeat, until all six sides of each block are covered with parts of six different puzzles.

This puzzle is made with photos of family and friends, but cut the photos so that you can make new faces by mixing the child's eyes with mommy's nose and daddy's chin — or invent a baby brother using the features of different members of the family.

To make this puzzle, select face-on shots of family and friends. The photos should be the same size and should fill almost the entire picture. After gluing the photos to stiff cardboard backing, cut each photo into three sections — the eyes, the nose, and the mouth. An interesting variation on this puzzle is to divide-up photos of animals to make strange, new animals.

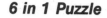

6 in 1 Puzzle

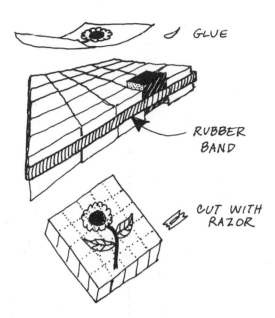

GLUE

RUBBER BAND

CUT WITH RAZOR

Reversal Puzzle

CUT
CUT

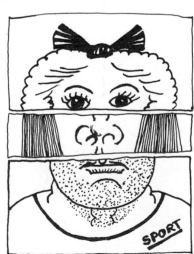

Jigsaw Puzzle   This puzzle, as the name implies, is most easily made with a jig saw. Glue an art print, photo, or map — whatever — to a thin board, such as a piece of masonite. Trace and use the pattern below, or just invent your own. Be sure to use a fine blade so that the edges of the paper will not tear.

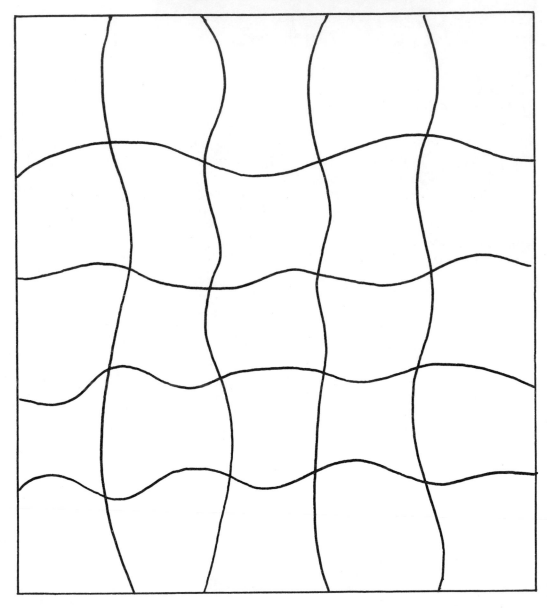

The bathtub puzzle is made of any smooth vinyl material — such as upholstery plastic — which adheres to the sides of the tub when wet. The fishes can be fit together or strung in lines and schools.

Bathtub Puzzle

Blocks

With blocks, it's not a case of what the toy can do, but of what the child can do with the toy. They are raw material for a kid's imagination. Blocks are a pretty good investment of your time and energy because they are of interest to a wide range of ages from the hold-and-suck stage onwards. Older kids begin to build definite forms which blossom into zoos, farms, ships sailing on the high seas, and futuristic cities.

Those of you struck with 'enrichment fever' might be gratified to know that blocks are considered (in lingo) to be basic learning tools which develop your child's sense of spatial relationships, promote the development of physical co-ordination, etc., etc. Be that as it may, these blocks are free, are relatively easy to make, and kids do like them.

Wood Scrap Blocks

Wood scrap blocks can be obtained free from your local lumber yard, any construction site, or a neighborhood do-it-yourself type. To be safe, you should sand all edges to get rid of sharp corners, and sand all surfaces until they are splinter free.

Giant Blocks

Giant blocks can be made from painted beer cases, soda crates and produce crates — all available free from your kindly liquor or grocery store. The produce crates come in two strengths; so look for the sturdier ones.

Empty thread spools and small scraps of wood make a fine table top block set.

Tiny Blocks

A fine storage box for all those blocks can be made by adding casters to a discarded packing crate. The wheels make it easy for the child to push the box around, and clean up after himself.

Block Box

When you pick up the casters, try to get the kind which mount with four bolts — the wood used in most of these crates is too thin to support standard casters.

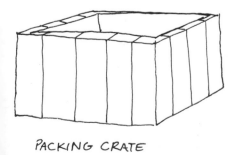

PACKING CRATE

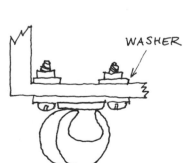

WASHER

Puppets

Early learning enthusiasts would say that puppets provide valuable experience in role-playing. Psychologists would say that puppets furnish kids with a constructive outlet for venting their hostilities. Parents would say that puppets keep kids busy. Kids would say puppets are fun. So it goes . . . Here's a bunch of puppets you can make. Some take only a few minutes; others take a bit more time and effort.

Finger Puppets

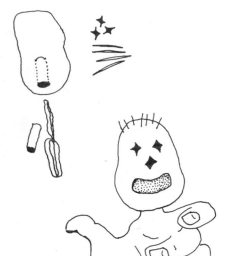

Pare a finger hole from an apple, potato or pear. Invent a face using cloves, beans, olives, orange peels, cherries, toothpicks, etc. When the kids are finished, let them wash the fruit off and eat 'em.

Kids can make these puppets by themselves. Draw and cut a figure out of construction paper; cut two small holes for fingers so that the puppet can walk.

Popsicle-Stick Puppets

Another do-it-yourselfer for kids. They cut out the heads, draw in faces, and glue them onto popsicle sticks. To make a popsicle stick puppet theatre, paint a scene on the inside of a tissue box, and cut a slit in the bottom to stick the puppets through.

There are zillions of ways to turn a paper bag into a puppet. Here are some of our favorites.

The little candy bags that penny candies come in can be used to make this quickie puppet. The middle finger comes through the nose hole and wiggles.

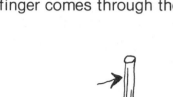

Affix a candy bag puppet face over a flashlite with a rubber band. Kids love to play with these in the dark.

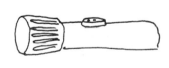

Draw this puppet's lips where the bag's bottom folds flat against the bag. The mouth then opens and shuts when the hand inside the bag moves the flap up and down.

Face Boards   Face boards are really hand held masks which you cut from cardboard. Make the mask about the same size as the kid's head, and cut out the eye holes.

Add faces to the front and back if you want to make them reversible for a quick change of characters. Kids might enjoy making characters from a favorite story and acting out the story. We did a grand production of "Where the Wild Things Are."

Body Boards   Body boards are an extension of the same idea. Stretch your child out on a piece of cardboard and mark the positions for the arm and head holes.

Cut out the arm and head holes, and decorate the board with bodies or figures.

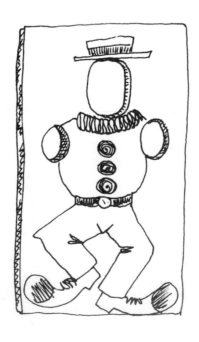 

Wash and dry a yogurt carton. Paint it and add a face. Fold an 11" x 11" scrap of material in half and sew up one side. Staple or glue one open end to the mouth of the carton. Glue on a bit of yarn or fluff for hair, and you've got a puppet.

Or, you can make a marionette by using a yogurt carton for the body, a spray paint can top for the head, and any arrangement of soda pop tops and large and small bottle tops and thread spools.

Cloth Puppet   A close friend named Caryn makes these lovely cloth puppets and sells them at local craft fairs. The body of the puppet requires only an 8" x 36" piece of heavy felt, and the jacket, an 8" x 10" piece. If you have access to a sewing machine (and even if you don't) you will find this puppet to be easy to assemble, and much loved.

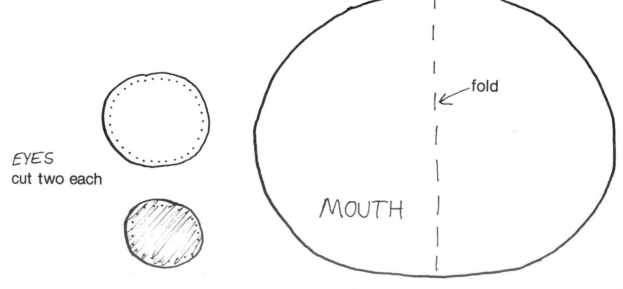

EYES
cut two each

fold

MOUTH

cut one of cloth, and cut one of thin cardboard

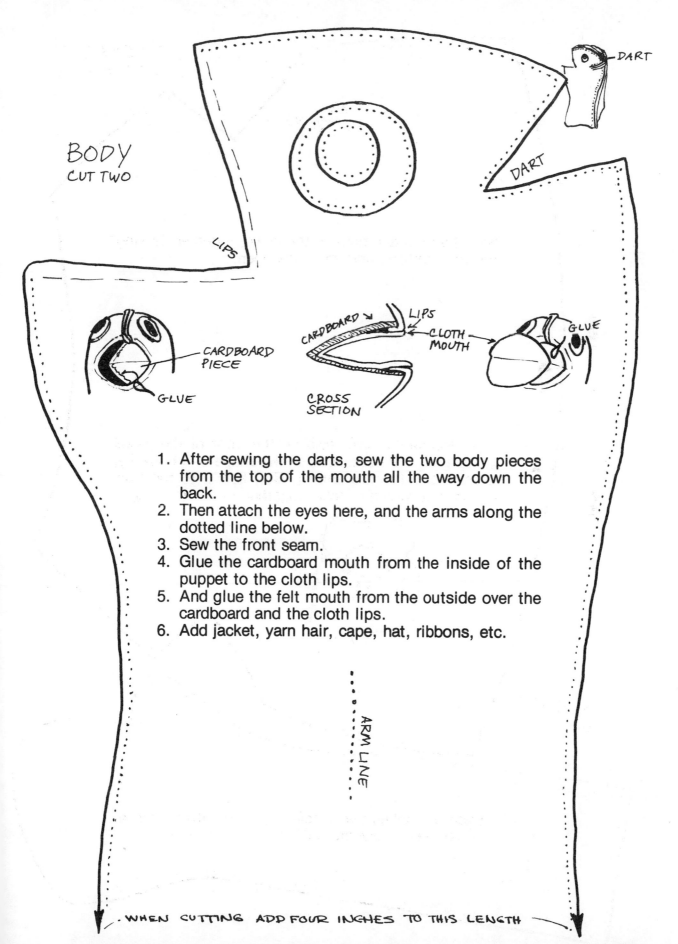

BODY
CUT TWO

DART

DART

LIPS

CARDBOARD PIECE

GLUE

CARDBOARD

LIPS

CLOTH MOUTH

GLUE

CROSS SECTION

1. After sewing the darts, sew the two body pieces from the top of the mouth all the way down the back.
2. Then attach the eyes here, and the arms along the dotted line below.
3. Sew the front seam.
4. Glue the cardboard mouth from the inside of the puppet to the cloth lips.
5. And glue the felt mouth from the outside over the cardboard and the cloth lips.
6. Add jacket, yarn hair, cape, hat, ribbons, etc.

ARM LINE

WHEN CUTTING ADD FOUR INCHES TO THIS LENGTH

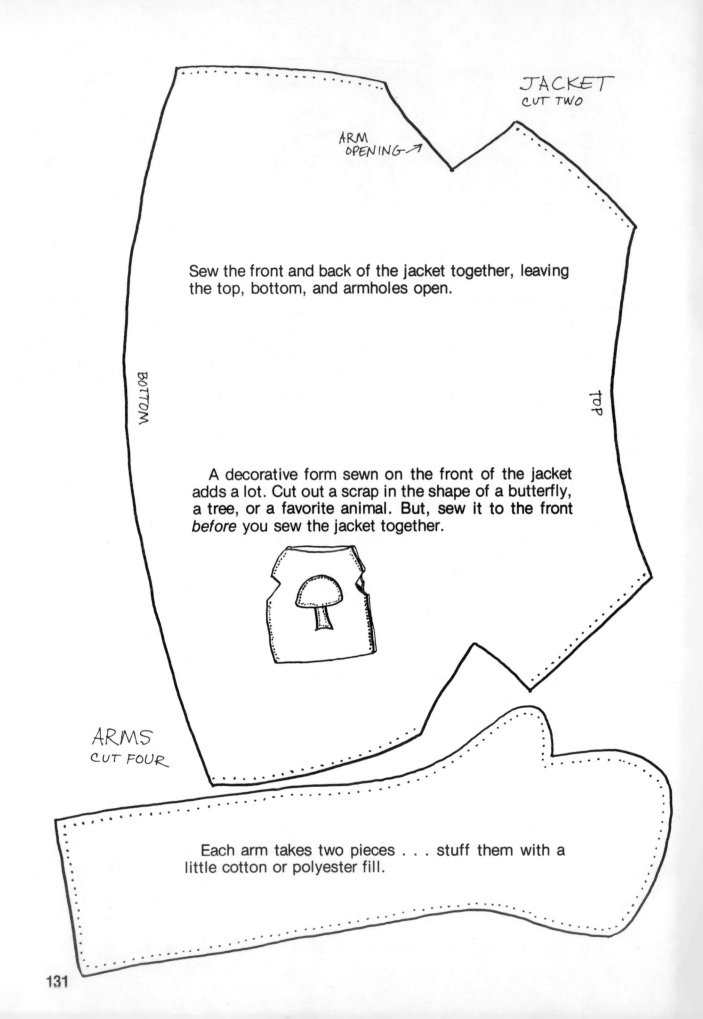

JACKET
CUT TWO

ARM
OPENING↗

Sew the front and back of the jacket together, leaving the top, bottom, and armholes open.

BOTTOM

TOP

A decorative form sewn on the front of the jacket adds a lot. Cut out a scrap in the shape of a butterfly, a tree, or a favorite animal. But, sew it to the front *before* you sew the jacket together.

ARMS
CUT FOUR

Each arm takes two pieces . . . stuff them with a little cotton or polyester fill.

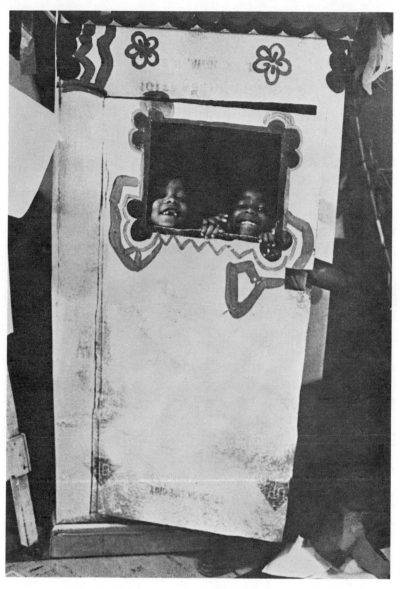

If your puppets lead to great drama, that might call for a puppet theatre. It can be as simple as cutting a hole in an old sheet and hanging it in the doorway. Or make a more deluxe theatre by cutting an opening in the side of a large appliance box for the stage, and add curtains and a bit of paint. A simple t.v. marionette theatre can be made from an open top box with a t.v. screen cut out in one side.

Puppet Theatres

Wooden Toys

Toys which are made of wood feel nice and tend to last a long time. Unfortunately, they are often expensive. The toys illustrated on these pages were all made from scraps found at a local lumber yard and odd pieces of board left over from some do-it-yourself projects. The dimensions given here are just suggestions. You will have to adjust them to the wood which is available to you.

Spool Racer

Here is a very simple wooden toy which moves under its own means of propulsion. Wind up its rubber band motor, set it down on a smooth surface, and watch it go.

To make one of your own, hammer two small nails into one end of a used thread spool. Loop a four-inch rubber band over the nails, and run it through the spool. Slip a short piece of ¼" dowel rod through the open loop of the rubber band, give the propeller a good twist, lay the spool racer on its side, and zoooooooooooooooom.

This little boat is propelled by a working paddle wheel. The hull is cut from a 4" x 8" piece of scrap. Cut your hull to a point at the bow, and cut out a piece 1½" deep, and 2¾" wide at the stern to accept the paddle. Place a rubber band over the paddle wheel as illustrated, through washers at each end, and over the notched arms of the hull. Glue on a wheel house, paint or varnish, wind the paddle up, and off you go.

Paddle Wheel Boats

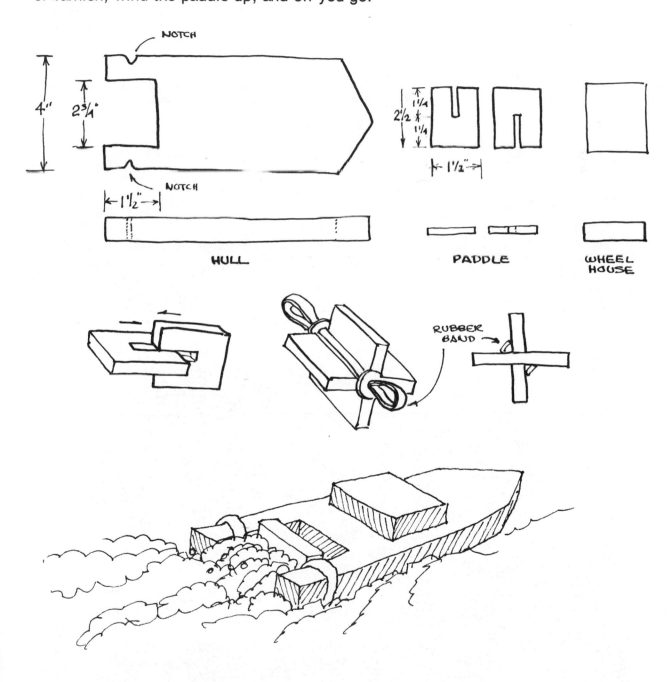

Doll House   This dollhouse requires a bit of effort, but I like it because it is so sturdy. Eric and Peter can play house while Jerry and Jenny climb on top. Since it is open on both sides, as many as four kids can play with it at a time. Depending on where you live, it can be an apartment house, a duplex, or a two-story home.

We made people for our doll house out of jumbo stringing beads that we found on sale at a toy store. By stacking the beads in various orders, we made big and little people of all colors. We held the people together by running a piece of wooden dowel covered with glue through the holes in the beads. To finish, we painted faces and hair on the beads.

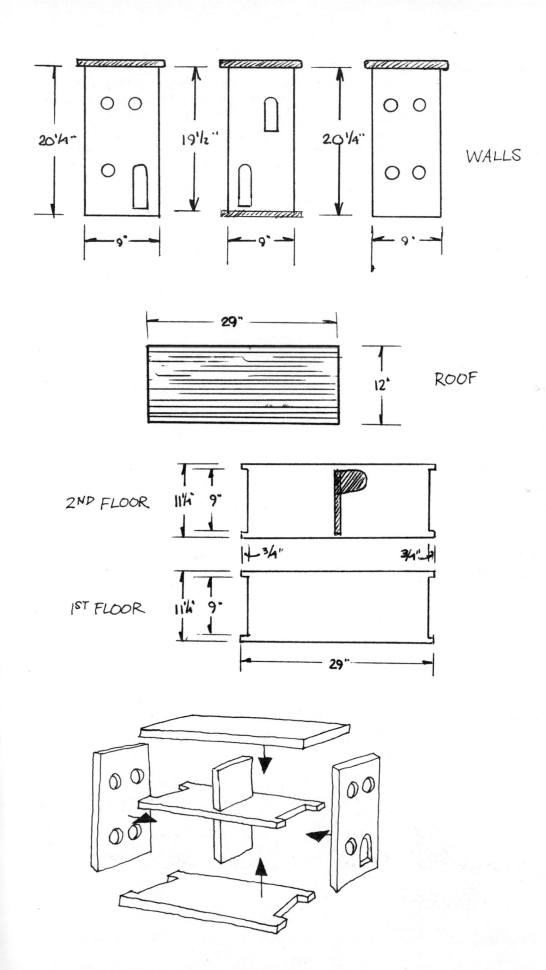

20¼" 19½" 20¼"

WALLS

9" 9" 9"

29"

12"

ROOF

2ND FLOOR 11¼" 9"

¾" ¾"

1ST FLOOR 11¼" 9"

29"

Scrapwood Fleets You don't have to be an accomplished carpenter to produce a whole fleet of cars, trucks and boats out of scrapwood. You can make your own wheels by cutting off ½" slices of a 1½" dowel rod, or by using a circular hole saw attachment on an electric drill — or just borrow some hubs from a Tinkertoy set. Here are some simple forms to start you off — your imagination and your materials will supply the inspiration for all sorts of vehicles.

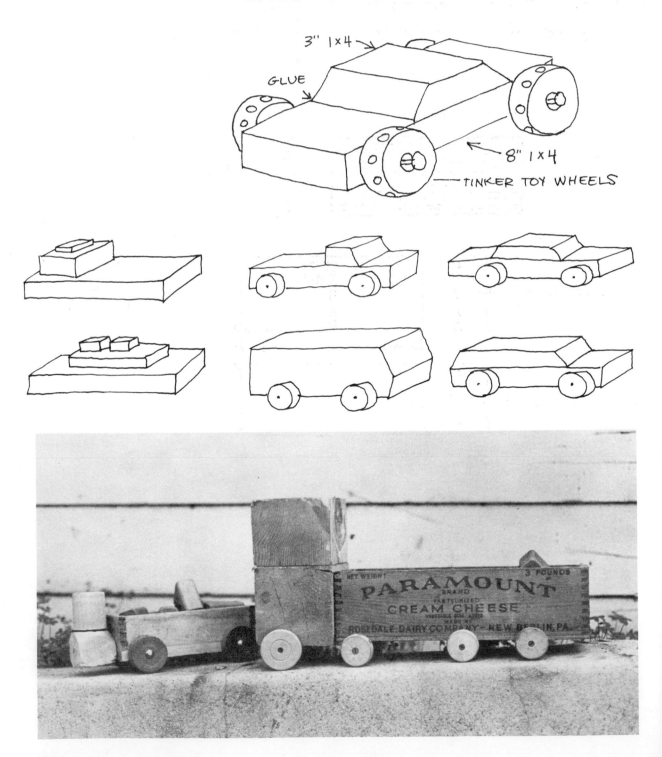

Sand and Water Toys

Every kid should have an opportunity to play in sand and splash in the water. Even if you are stuck in the middle of the city surrounded by concrete, there's always a nook or crannie for a sandbox. Take an old tub, cheap dime store swimming pool, or baby's bathtub and fill it with sand. If you have a yard for the kids to play in, sand makes a good ground cover, and can be purchased cheaply from building supply companies.

Sand screens can be made by attaching small pieces of screen to very simple wooden frames. Make several using different kinds of screen, from one-half-inch square mesh down through window screen.

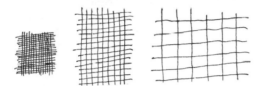

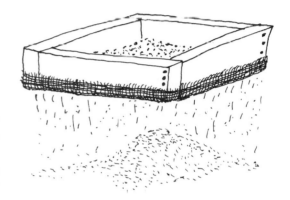

In warm weather a cheap pool or old wash tub provide endless hours of water fun — or simply set up a hose and sprinkler. Provide corks, plastic measuring cups, tubes, plastic straws, spoons, egg beaters, plastic lemons, and other unbreakable floating objects for water play. Of course, kids need constant supervision when they're playing around water.

Any discarded plastic container with a molded handle can be transformed into a pail and a combination scoop/funnel. Merely cut the bottle about three-quarters of an inch below the handle and presto — sand and water toys. If the edges are too sharp, use coarse sand paper or a file to blunt them.

Pail/Scoop/Funnel

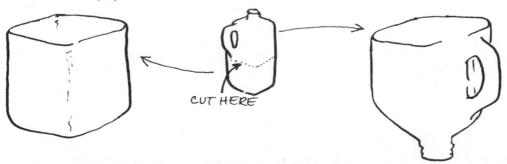

CUT HERE

Educational Toys

So-called "educational toys" are a big business. Toy manufacturers have been quick to cash in on the current interest in pre-school education by labeling all sorts of toys "educational" and by marketing over-priced "scientifically-designed" and "educator-approved" toys. Actually, all toys are educational in the sense that children learn from them. In this sense, a set of blocks is an educational toy. But some toys are educational in a more specific sense. Maria Montessori is, perhaps, the grandmother of this kind of educational toy. Around the turn of this century, Montessori, a woman doctor discouraged by the prejudice against women in her profession, turned her attention to mentally retarded children. Working with these children, and later with children from the slums of Rome, she developed a philosophy of education, and designed special educational apparatus that children could use to teach themselves.

These toys make use of a child's tactile, olfactory, auditory and visual senses. Unlike a set of blocks, which is an "open ended" toy, this type of toy is much more specific. They present a problem or lesson which the child solves or discovers through playing with the toy. These educational toys are more limited in the play opportunities they present, but can teach specific skills. Because of their expense and limited usefulness, they are often not as valuable as some of the more open-ended toys.

On the next few pages, you will find directions for making some of the more valuable educational toys. These toys will help to develop eye-hand coordination, the small muscles used in writing, and the abilities of judging relative sizes, classifying, and perceiving logical sequences.

Children develop many of these skills quite naturally in their play. Many of these toys recreate activities that your kids already encounter in the course of their day. You needn't force or coax your kid to play with these toys, although they will probably be delighted with your efforts.

When playing with these toys with your child, use words which will help to expand vocabulary. Let the kids make the rules and decide on how to make use of the toys you've made. Don't insist on the "correct" way." Make suggestions; ask questions. Let the kids discover the ideas and relationships which are implicit in the materials. But most importantly: play with your children, and be lavish with your praise.

Shape Sorting

The shape sorting box is a real classic — often used in I.Q. tests. Kids discover that you can't fit a round peg through a square hole. A shoe box whose lid is cut with holes to fit any available blocks provides an inexpensive version. If there are no blocks which will serve, cut your own from tagboard.

Nuts & Bolts

This is a game where kids exercise their ability to judge relative sizes in order to find what fits with what. Screwing the nuts onto the matching bolts helps to exercise the fingers and develop manual dexterity. We glued the bolts to a block of wood to provide a solid base. To really educate your senses, try doing this task blindfolded.

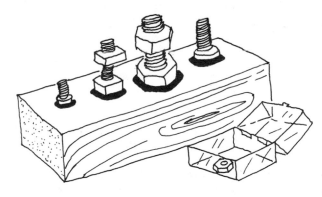

Lotto

Lotto is a matching game with endless variations: colors, textures, patterns, numbers, words, animals and their habitats, people and occupations, etc. To make a color lotto, take a square of wood, divide it into nine sections, and paint each section a different color. Then make a set of nine cards of the same size and color as the sections on the board. You might also print the names of the colors on the boards. The kids can play alone or in a group — throw in a spinner or dice and let them invent their own rules for a game.

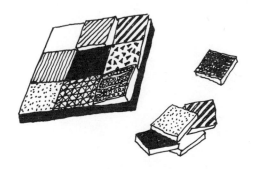

Cylinders   Graduated cylinders can be made from a mailing tube cut into various lengths — 4", 5", 6", etc. Watch to see when your kid gets around to lining them up from shortest to tallest.

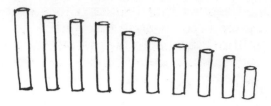

Flannel Boards   Flannel boards can be used all sorts of ways. You can cut out shapes, numbers, letters. Kids can count, form sets, learn basic shapes and color names, make words, and create designs, stories and funny faces.

The board is merely a piece of wood or sturdy cardboard covered with a piece of flannel. Any small piece of felt will stick to the board; as will pictures cut from magazines when rubbed with sandpaper, or backed with felt. Some kids love to put on flannel board shows and make up their own stories.

Patterns   This game helps kids to recognize and reproduce patterns. All that is needed is a small set of colored blocks of different size and shape, and a few cards with different patterns. At first, they can set the shapes directly on the cards. Later, they can reproduce the patterns alongside, or without directly referring to the cards.

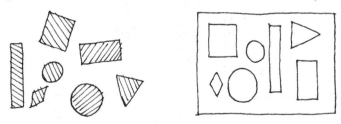

Stack & Nest   Another classic. A set of cans or boxes which fit inside one another — or which can be stacked to build towers. They can be as simple as 1#, 2#, and 3# coffee cans, or as fancy as handcrafted wooden boxes.

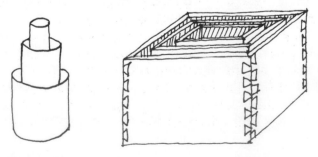

For this game, make a board like the one shown here, and a set of cards that the kids can sort onto the board according to whether they are the same or not. A friend made an excellent version of this game with several ambiguous cards, like two balloons of different shape . . . Were they the same, or were they different? She also made a card with twin girls — one with pigtails and the other with braids. All of the kids, and none of the adults, noticed the difference.

Same/Different

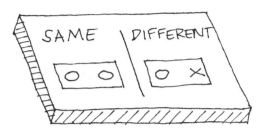

You can purchase fancy teaching aids to assist children in "learning how to judge relative sizes and develop matching skills," or pull out your pots and lids, and let them match the lids to the pots. Empty jars and lids also help to "develop eye-hand coordination" — but be careful of glass jars that might break.

Pots & Lids

Maria Montessori used similar frames in her work. To make this version, mount two pieces of heavy fabric (with clothing fasteners attached) to a board. Be sure to leave enough slack in the material so that the fasteners can be worked easily.

Dressing Frames

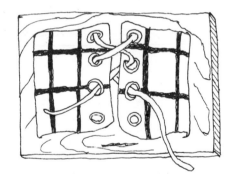

Another "eye-hand coordination developer." For the novitiate, provide empty thread spools and shoelaces. For the more coordinated, try stringing macaroni. Painting the spools or macaroni brightens up the strings considerably.

Stringing Beads

Round up an empty egg carton and a supply of buttons of assorted colors, sizes and shapes. Let the kids decide how to sort the buttons — by size, color number of holes — whatever. (Be sure that the child involved has passed the 'stick everything in your mouth' stage.)

Button Sorting

Our culture is visually oriented — we rely heavily upon our eyes for information about our world. But we have other senses as well. These games emphasize some of those other sensitivities.

Sound Cans Fill two sets of metal film cans with small objects like bells, rice, pennies, etc. Seal well with cloth tape. Try to match the cans that sound the same.

Feely Boxes Feely boxes let kids tune in their sense of touch. Seal the top and bottom of a cardboard box and cut two holes in one end so the kids can stick their hands in. Fill the feely box with squares of burlap, silk, velvet, and other textured materials. Paste duplicate squares of each on top of the box, and let them feel for the matching material. Feely boxes can also be used with shapes:

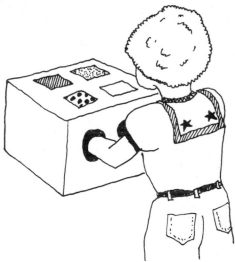

Weight Cartons The object of this game is to match up cartons that weigh the same. To make the game, use two sets of milk or juice cartons. Fill each pair of cartons with varying amounts of sand or plaster of paris — i.e., ¼ cup, ½ cup, ⅔ cup, etc., and seal tightly.

Smelly Jars For this game you need some jars with lids. (Baby food jars will do nicely.) After painting the jars so that you can't see inside, put a piece of gauze soaked with something smelly inside each jar. Use cinnamon, rose essence, lemon, peppermint, peanut butter, Vick's Vaporub, etc. Then, make a set of cards with pictures of a lemon, a jar of peanut butter, a Vick's label, and so forth. Let the kids match the jars with the labels.

Appendix

Processing Film

Equipment and Materials

1. Film Developing Tank
   We bought an Ansco tank which has an adjustable reel (A) that can accommodate 120, 126, 127 and 35mm film. The tank comes with a thermometer (D), another necessary piece of equipment, which also serves as handle for turning the film reel during processing. The exposed film is loaded onto the reel in *complete* darkness. The reel is then placed inside the tank (B) and the lid(C) is locked on. The rest of the process can be done under normal lighting conditions. If you are developing sheet film you will not use a tank. Instead, you will use three trays which are large enough to hold a sheet of film. The process for developing sheet and roll film is essentially the same, but a safelight is used while developing sheet film. The film package will tell you what type of safelight to use. Except for the safelight, the room must remain completely light-tight during sheet film developing.

2. Kitchen timer or clock, preferably with a second hand. Three different chemicals are poured in and out of the developing tank during processing. Timing is critical. If the film spends too long or short a time in the solutions it will not yield good negatives.

3. Clothespins, paper clasps or film clips. These will hold the film as it dries.

4. Storage bottles for chemicals. If possible these should be dark glass or plastic so that light will not deteriorate the chemicals. Label the bottles, keep them tightly stopped and store in a dark place out of the reach of youngsters. Each chemical you use has a certain capacity which is indicated on the mixing instructions. On the bottle lable, keep a record of how many rolls of film or sheets of paper you have processed so that you will know when the chemical is exhausted.*

5. Chemicals:
    a. developer — Film is coated with silver bromide crystals which are sensitive to light. The developer helps convert the crystals on the exposed film to metallic silver. The areas of the film struck by the most light are darkened by the silver metal, while the areas where no light has struck remain transparent. The intermediate areas have varying amounts of silver, creating shades of gray. There are many developers available. We use Kodak's D-76. There are also some developers which can be used for both film and paper. Ask the sales person at your store to recommend one for you.
    b. stop bath — Stop bath, as the name implies, stops the action of the developer. Although water can be used I prefer stop bath since kids are sometimes slow at pouring chemicals in and out of the tank. The stop bath action is immediate. We use Kodak's Stop Bath with Indicator that turns purplish when the bath is exhausted.
    c. fixer — This solution "fixes" the image on the film so that it is no longer subject to fading when exposed to light. We use Kodak's Rapid Fix which can be used for film and, when diluted, for paper as well.

*Many times capacity is given in terms of number of 8" x 10" sheets per gallon of solution that can be processed before the chemical is exhausted. Two rolls of 127 film are equal to one sheet of 8" x 10" paper; 7 rolls of 126 equal two 8" x 10" sheets; 1 roll of 120 equals one 8" x 10" sheet.

Step 1: Loading the Film   The first step should be done by an adult in *complete* darkness (inside a closet, under a heavy blanket). The film can or cartridge must be pried open. A beer opener will help here. If the film you use has a paper backing, this backing must be removed. The film tank will come with loading instructions. With most plastic tanks you will slip the end of the film under a clip and rotate the reel back and forth. The reel has a mechanism which catches on the film sprockets and pulls them into the reel. You may find it necessary to practice loading a processed roll of film before trying it in the dark. Adjust the reel to your film size and roll the film onto the reel. After the film is loaded on the reel, placed in the tank and the lid is on, the rest of the steps can be carried out in normal light. With sheet film, you will continue to work with only the specified safelight.

Step 2: Developing   Now you are ready to add the developer. Timing is crucial. The length of time that the film should spend in the developer depends on the size and type of film, the kind of developer and the temperature of the developer. The chart below gives temperature and times for 127 verichrome pan film using D-76. If you use another film or developer, be sure to check instructions that come with the film for correct development time.

Temperature	Time
65°	8 minutes
68°	7 minutes
70°	6 minutes, 15 seconds
72°	5 minutes, 45 seconds
75°	5 minutes

Most developers work best at about 68°. You can adjust the temperature of your chemicals by setting them in cooler or warmer water for 5 minutes or so.

Once you have figured out the correct time, set the timer and pour the proper amount of developer into the film tank. For 127 film in the Ansco tank use 12 ounces of developer (enough to cover the film). Check the instructions that come with your tank for the amount of solution to use. After the developer is in the tank, turn the timer on.

Then, rap the tank gently on the table or countertop a few times to dislodge air bubbles. To insure consistent development it is necessary to agitate the film. Methods of agitation vary. I agitate constantly for the first 15 seconds and then once every minute for about 5 seconds each time. To agitate, turn the handle/thermometer that protrudes through the tank lid clockwise and counterclockwise two or three times. With sheet film, you agitate by gently rocking the tray of developing solution. When developing time is up, pour the developer back in the storage bottle.

As soon as the developer is poured out, pour the correct amount of stop bath into the tank. Agitate constantly for 30 seconds. The temperature of the stop bath is not as critical, but it should be within 10° of the developer temperature. After 30 seconds, pour the stop bath back into the storage bottle.

Step 3: Stop Bath

Pour the correct amount of fixer into your tank. Most fixers require 5-10 minutes of fixing. Agitate during fixing just as you did in developing. Again the temperature should be about the same as the developer. Once the fixer has been poured back into its storage bottle, the tank can be opened.

Step 4: Fixing

Set the film tank under a faucet of running water and allow it to wash for at least 30 minutes. You can use one of several chemicals to shorten washing time. We use Hustler Rapid Bath.

Step 5: Washing

If you agitate the film in a solution of Hustler for 30 seconds after fixing, you can cut wash time to 4 minutes. The water temperature should be 65°-70°. Prolonged washing in colder or warmer water may result in damage to the film's emulsion or incomplete washing.

We also use Kodak's Photo-Flo after the wash to prevent water spots. Simply dip the film in the Photo-Flo and allow it to drain. Both the Rapid Bath and Photo-Flo are optional.

After the film is washed, clip a clothespin or plastic clasp to one end and unroll the film from the reel. Hang the strip of negatives to dry. It is important that the film be hung in a place where it will not touch anything and where there is a minimum of dust and moving air currents. After the film is completely dry cut into 3 or 4 strips and store in glassine negative holders or in an envelope.

Step 6: Drying

Contact Printing

1. a clean piece of 8" x 10" cardboard or wood

2. an 8" x 10" sheet of window pane glass (about 75¢)

3. a gooseneck lamp with a 25 watt bulb

4. a candle

5. a timer or clock with a second hand

6. rubber gloves or 3 tongs

7. four 8" x 10" trays for chemicals and washing—these must be at least 8" x 10"; they may be larger. We have used glass baking dishes, but they must be perfectly clean to avoid contamination of chemicals. The inexpensive disposable, heavy-duty foil pans sold for holiday turkeys will do nicely. Label the trays "developer," "stop," "fixer," and "wash."

8. chemicals:
   a. developer—we use Nacco's Printol, which can also be used for film. Dilute according to instructions for projection papers. For best results the temperature should be about 68°, but it will work at lower or higher temperatures.
   b. stop bath—same solution used for negatives
   c. fixer—we use Rapid Fix, diluted twice as much as for film developing.

9. photographic paper—there are many types of paper available. We use Kodabrome RC (#2 or #3) because it is coated with a special resin that allows the paper to dry in five minutes without curling; this eliminates the need for flattening solutions, rollers, print dryers, or blotting pads. It costs about $4.50 for 25 sheets.

D-9543
5-19

Photographic paper is not as sensitive to light as film. Still, you will need to work in the dark. The only light you should have is a Kodak safelight or a small candle set about 5 feet from your working area. This will enable you to see without affecting the paper. light will enable you to see, but it will not affect the paper.

Position your piece of cardboard or wood under the gooseneck lamp so that the light from the lamp covers the entire piece of cardboard. Set out your trays of developer, stop bath, fixer and water in a row near the lamp.

Step 1: Set-up*

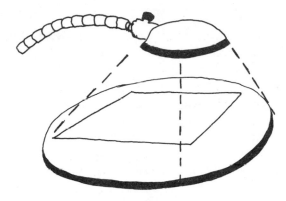

Next, you must test your darkroom to make sure that it is really dark enough and that the candle is not too bright. Blow out your candle. Allow your eyes to adjust to the darkness. If you are reasonably sure that the room is light-tight, open your package of photo paper. Reach inside, being careful not to expose all the paper to the untested room, and tear off a corner of one piece of paper. Allow your scrap to sit for a minute or so. Then place it in the developer for a minute. Lift it out, let it drain and place in the stop bath for 30 seconds. Finally, place the scrap in the fixer. After it has been in the fixer for about one minute, you may turn on the lights. If the scrap is still white, your room is light-tight.

Now, you may check for the candle's brightness. Pull out another scrap of paper and place it under your 8" x 10" piece of cardboard. Light the candle. Then place the scrap of paper on top of the cardboard for a minute. Move the scrap through the three baths again. After it has been in the fixer for a minute, turn

Step 2: Testing the Darkroom

*The set up described here is for roll film, if you are using sheet film, the process is essentially the same. If you have paper negatives from a pin hole camera, use the paper negative just as if it were a piece of film and use the same kind of photographic paper for the print.

on the lights. If the paper is darkened at all, it means that the candle is too bright. Move the candle further away and repeat the process again until your scrap of paper shows no darkening.

Step 3: Test Strips

Now you are ready to make some test strips. In your dark room, open the photo paper package and take out one sheet. Cut it into three or four strips lengthwise. Take one of the strips and lay it emulsion (shiny) side up on the 8" x 10" piece of cardboard. Put the other strips back in the package. Take a strip of negatives and lay it on top of the strip of photo paper so that the emulsion side of your negative (the dull side) is touching the paper. Lay your sheet of glass on top of the negative and paper. Turn on the lamp for 10 seconds. Then take the photo paper from under the glass and negatives and place it in the developer. After about one minute you should see the positive or print. The edges should be black, and the print itself should have white, gray and black areas.

If the print is too dark, the paper is overexposed. Make another test strip, using less exposure to the light. If the print is too light or gray in color, make another strip with a longer exposure to light. It is possible that the negatives themselves are under/over exposed or developed. If you have problems like this, or with any other stage of the process, get a copy of *How to Develop, Print and Enlarge Pictures* by S. Epstein and De Armand (Amphoto, New York, 1970; $1.95), which is an excellent book for beginners.

Step 4: Contact Printing

Once you have determined the proper exposure time, you are ready to make your contact print. Remove a sheet of photo paper and place it on the cardboard, shiny side up. Place the negative strips on the top of the paper—emulsion (dull) side touching the emulsion (shiny) side of the photo paper. Set the glass on top of the negatives and paper. Turn the light on for the proper exposure time.

Remove the photo paper and place in the developing bath until the print looks good to you (about 1 minute). Prints will dry a bit lighter than they look when wet; so take this into consideration. The print should be agitated slightly while in the developer to make sure all the areas are equally developed. Then put the print into the stop bath for 30 seconds—again with agitation. Finally, put the print into the fixer for 5-10 minutes. After it has been in the fixer for about a minute, you may turn on the lights and inspect the print.

When I work in the darkroom by myself, I use my fingers to move the print from one tray to another, but it is not good practice. The chemicals are poisonous and kids have a tendency to put their fingers in their mouths. Also, mixing the stop bath or fixer with the developer will ruin the developer. For these reasons, move the prints with tongs, using a separate set of tongs for each chemical. On occasion, I have also used rubber gloves, but rinse them off after the fixer and before touching the developer again.

After the print has been fixed, it should be washed. We wash prints, one or two at a time, in a tray set in the bath tub. Keep a strong stream of water running from the tap so that the prints will wash well. To make sure that the prints are washed well, we usually agitate them for 2 minutes in a tray of Hustler Rapid Bath (the same solution used for negatives). Wash them in running water for about 10 minutes. If you do not use Hustler, wash prints for an hour. The water temperature should be between 65°-70° to insure complete washing.

Step 5: Washing and Drying

After washing simply set the print on a clean, flat surface, blot with a piece of paper and let them dry. Prints will dry in about 5 minutes, using the resin-coated paper. If you use non-coated paper, you will need a print dryer or a blotting pad because non-resin papers often curl. The resin paper costs about 4¢ a sheet more, but it's worth the extra money.